Trust :: Data

A New Framework for Identity and Data Sharing

Edited by
Thomas Hardjono, David Shrier and Alex Pentland

www.visionaryfuture.com

Trust :: Data
A New Framework for Identity and Data Sharing

VISIONARY FUTURE

www.VisionaryFuture.com

Portions of this work were previously published; reproduced with permission of the authors.

EDITED BY:

Thomas Hardjono, David Shrier and Alex Pentland

Acknowledgements

To our children, who inspire us
to build a better tomorrow.

CONTENTS

INTRODUCTION

Trust :: Data

Thomas Hardjono, David Shrier and Alex Pentland

SOCIETY'S NERVOUS SYSTEM

An earlier version of this chapter appeared in IEEE Computer, January 2012, authored by Alex Pentland

We and our colleagues at the Massachusetts Institute of Technology are trying to invent the future. It's not enough, in our view, to simply assess or analyze the existing state of the world, or even to forecast trends. For us, we want to create tools, frameworks and help build consensus to build a better tomorrow.

In the realm of data, personal privacy, and information security, it's easy to identify problems but difficult to find effective solutions. Governments are increasingly aware of the costs and risks associated with the current state and the need for an improved future state.

This book will take you through our current thinking about technologies and approaches that can better manage identity, better protect personal information and improve how it is used, and better protect critical data from attack. We will then explore some of the implications of a "New Deal on Data" and the value people place on personal information, including the legal and policy implications. Finally, we will discuss how implementing these various technologies in a coherent system is being tested through a series of "Living Labs" that we are building around the world in places ranging from Trento, Italy to Bogota, Colombia.

Building Trust in Government, Energy, and Public Health Data Systems

It's helpful to appreciate context on motivations and frameworks for data systems we can trust, and even data systems that build trust. Sustaining a healthy, safe, and efficient society is a challenge that goes back to the 1800s, when the Industrial Revolution spurred rapid urban growth and created huge social and environmental problems. The remedy then was to engineer centralized networks that delivered clean water and safe food, removed waste, provided energy, facilitated transportation, and offered access to centralized healthcare, police, and educational services.

These century-old solutions are increasingly obsolete. Today's social structures are not designed as integrated systems and do not take advantage of new digital feedback technologies that would allow them to be dynamic and responsive.

We need to radically rethink our approach. Rather than separate systems by function—water, food, waste, transport, education, energy, and so on—we must consider them holistically. Instead of focusing only on access and distribution systems, we need dynamic, networked, self-regulating systems that take into account complex interactions. In short, to ensure a sustainable future society, we must use evolving technologies to create a nervous system for humanity that maintains the stability of government, energy, and public health systems around the globe.

The central idea is to reinvent societal systems within a real-time, proactive framework: sense the situation, combine observations with dynamic demand and reaction models, and use the resulting predictions to update the system. Fortunately, much of the sensing and many of the required updating elements are already in place. What is missing, though, are the dynamic interaction models along with a trusted data architecture that guarantees safety, stability, and efficiency.

The required models must describe human demands and reactions, as people are at the core of all these systems. Consequently, we must observe individual behavior, which creates an exponential growth in personal data. Meglena Kuneva, the European Commissioner for Consumer Protection in 2007-2010, highlighted the importance of such data when she described it as "the new oil of the Internet and the new currency of the digital world" [1].

One consequence of this growth in behavior-sensing data is that the architecture of future systems must also guarantee privacy and fair treatment for all potential participants. As Jon Leibowitz, chairman of the US Federal Trade Commission, declared, "privacy and security protections [must be built] into company procedures, systems, and technologies at the outset, so that they are an integral part of a company's business model"[2].

Realizing that using pervasive and mobile sensing to reinvent our society's infrastructure will require buy-in from citizens, government, and companies alike, in 2007 Alex Pentland proposed a "New Deal on Data"[3] to the World Economic Forum (WEF) and began a multiyear conversation involving the leaders of several major IT, wireless, infrastructure, and financial firms, as well as the heads of various international regulatory organizations and nongovernmental organizations. (The New Deal on Data is explained in more detail in

Chapter 4.) These discussions led to the formation of the *Rethinking Personal Data* project (www.weforum.org/ issues/rethinking-personal-data) the following year and, in 2011, to the publication of *Personal Data: The Emergence of a New Asset Class,* which described the growing consensus around the New Deal on Data and offered insights about the path forward [4] (See Appendix A).

PERVASIVE SENSING

Perhaps the prime example of personal data that is both extremely valuable to society, and simultaneously is among the most sensitive data that has become ubiquitous in the last decade, consider the location data generated by mobile telephones.

There are now over 5 billion mobile phone users worldwide, with millions of new subscribers every day. For the first time in history, most of humanity is linked and has a voice. More importantly, however, mobile phones are location-aware sensor platforms connected to wireless networks that support sensors where we live and work and in our modes of transportation. Consequently, our mobile wireless infrastructure can be "reality mined" to understand the patterns of human behavior, monitor our environments, and plan social development. Such functionality is mostly latent at this point, but researchers are already using it to measure urban migration, map population movements during natural disasters and emergencies, track disease outbreaks, identify neighborhoods with inadequate social services, and manage vehicular traffic congestion[3].

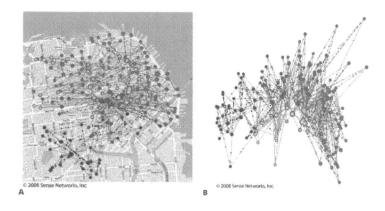

Figure 1.a and b

Figure 1. Figure 1a shows mobility patterns within a city, based on GPS data from mobile phones, color coded by common patterns of movement among restaurants, entertainment venues, and so on. As Figure 1b shows, the patterns reveal distinct population subgroups. Behavior stratification typically provides much more accurate predictions of people's risk for certain diseases (such as diabetes), consumer preferences, financial risks, and political views than standard demographics. It has also demonstrated great potential to improve public heath, urban planning, disaster response, and public education[4].

Data ownership and privacy

Perhaps the greatest challenges posed by pervasive sensing systems relate to data ownership and privacy [3]. Advances in network data analysis must balance creating value for data owners with protecting users' privacy.

This data must not become the exclusive domain either of private companies, in which case it will not contribute to the common good, or of the government, which will not serve the public interest of transparency. Similarly, we should enforce the use of anonymous data and, when possible, aggregate results. Robust collaboration and data sharing models must guard both consumers' privacy and corporations' competitive interests.

Private organizations collect the vast majority of personal data—in the form of location patterns, financial transactions, phone and Internet communications, and so on—and consequently will be key players in negotiations about data privacy and ownership. Both government regulation and market mechanisms will be needed to entice owners to share the data they gather while serving the interests of individuals and society at large.

New Deal on Data

Just as with financial and commodity markets, the first step toward creating an information market is to define ownership rights. This is why the subtitle of the WEF report refers to personal data as "a new asset class"[4].

The simplest approach to defining what it means to "own your own data" is to draw an analogy with the English common law tenets of possession, use, and disposal:

- You have the right to possess data about you. Regardless of what entity collects the data, the data belongs to you, and you can access it at any time. Data collectors thus play a role akin to a bank, managing the data on behalf of their "customers."

- You have the right to full control over the use of your data.
  The terms of use must be opt-in and clearly explained in plain
  language. If you are not happy with the way a company uses your
  data, you can remove it—just as you would close your account with
  a bank that is not providing satisfactory service.

- You have the right to dispose of or distribute your data. You have
  the option to destroy data about you or redeploy it elsewhere.

We will expand on these concepts in Chapter 4, but briefly:
Individual ownership of personal data must be balanced with the
need of corporations and governments to use certain data—account
activity, billing information, and so on—to run their day-to-day
operations. The proposed New Deal on Data therefore gives
individuals the right to possess, control, and dispose of these data as
well as all the other incidental data collected about you.

Enforcing the New Deal on Data

Enforcing personal data ownership rights goes beyond simply
authenticating an individual's identity; rather, it involves validating
whole series of "claims" and "privileges" of an individual, institution, or
even device to access and use such data. As more business, financial,
and govern mental services collect and use personal data, the
integrity and interoperability of a global authentication and "claims"
infrastructure will become paramount.

Because no single authority can micromanage all transactions,
failures, and attacks, such a global infrastructure—like the Internet
itself—must be highly distributed and user-centric to assure rapid
innovation, containment, and self-correction. The trust networks

or trust frameworks used by organizations such as Open Identity Exchange (OIX) are an example of such a distributed authority and are accepted not only by major companies but also many governments as well.

Similar to the ecosystems such as the OIX for identity federation, a trust network for personal data will need to continuously monitor, flag, and contain fraudulent and deceptive behavior. This will require innovations not only in software to track and audit activity in transaction networks, but also in policy and contract law to ensure simple, fair, and effective enforcement and remedies. MIT's OPAL/ENIGMA project has been formed by MIT Connection Science to develop a prototype of such a trust network in support of the WEF's Rethinking Personal Data project, and will test how trust networks perform "in the wild" (http://trust.mit.edu). Chapters 2 and 3 go into more detail on the constituent parts of OPAL/ENIGMA.

As authentication and claims processing becomes fully automated, legal and administrative processes should like-wise become more efficient, transparent, and accountable. In short, digital technologies should not only expedite the creation of a global infrastructure for highly reliable and innovative claims processing, but also eliminate much of the uncertainty, cost, and friction of legal and regulatory oversight. This would greatly diminish transaction costs and give rise to new forms of liquidity and innovative businesses. Given that verifiable trust reduces transaction risks and builds customer loyalty, it will be in the economic interest of those offering future online and mobile services to brand themselves as verifiable trusted stewards of personal data.

The Wild Wild Web

We have so far emphasized the new, sensor-derived sources of personal data because the extent and nature of this data is unfamiliar to many people, but of course massive amounts of personal data are already on the Web. Most of this data consists of information contributed by users to social network sites, blogs, and forums; transaction and registration data from online merchants and organizations; and browsing and click-stream histories. Researchers are just starting to reality mine user- contributed images and video, which, although consciously contributed, present many of the same challenges as passively collected sensor data such as call records and phone location data.

The Web evolved in an unregulated environment with no coherent privacy standards about personal data. Consequently, the rights to such data are unclear and vary from site to site. Location data, medical sensor data, and the like are collected by heavily regulated industries with fairly clear data ownership rules and could be made more widely accessible by extending the New Deal on Data to existing frameworks. But what of the Wild Wild Web? Fortunately, existing Web companies are coming under pressure to conform to the higher standards imposed on regulated industries.

This pressure is slowly causing progress. For instance, Google, following the initial round of WEF-led discussions that led to the Rethinking Personal Data project, released Google Dashboard (www.google.com/dashboard), which lets users know what data it has about them.

After a second round of discussions, the company formed the Data Liberation Front (www.dataliberation.org), a group of engineers whose mission statement is that "users should be able to control the data they store in any of Google's products" and whose goal is to "make it easier to move data in and out."

These new tools have the potential to make George Orwell's dystopian vision of an all-controlling state a reality. Consequently, we must think carefully about the growth and increasingly broad usage of personal data to drive societal systems, and particularly about the safety, stability, and fairness of their design.

Current legal statutes lag far behind our ability to collect and process data about people; clearly our notions of privacy and ownership of data must adapt to these new technologies. Perhaps the first step is to give people ownership of their data and guarantee what are called "fair information practices" for the data that is becoming the new global currency. It is time to draw on our rich legacy of thinking about the distribution and regulation of financial wealth to build societal systems that live up to our aspirations by being both equitable and efficient. Chapters 4 and 5 offers reflections on privacy and law in the new digital age.

The proposed New Deal on Data ensures accountability and data ownership, and we have successfully argued for its adoption by government, industry, and NGO leaders. Chapter 6 and 7 illustrates how the various elements described here can be piloted in a cohesive real-world system, a "Living Lab" for a new form of society.

If we can successfully address these challenges, current systems will evolve into an effective nervous system for our society, one that could repay our investment many-fold in terms of better civic services, a greener way of life, and a safer, healthier population.

CHAPTER 1

Towards the Internet of Trusted Data

Alex Pentland, David Shrier, Thomas Hardjono,
Irving Wladawsky-Berger

Summary of recommendations to the White House Commission on Cybersecurity from July 2016 meeting at MIT with senior executives from AT&T, IBM, MasterCard, Qualcomm, and U.S. Departments of Treasury and Commerce.

EXECUTIVE SUMMARY

As the economy and society move from a world where interactions were physical and based on paper documents, toward a world that is primarily governed by digital data and digital transactions, our existing methods of managing identity and data security are proving inadequate. Large-scale fraud, identity theft and data breaches are becoming common, and a large fraction of the population have only the most limited digital credentials. Even so, our Digital Infrastructure is recognized as a Strategic National Asset which must be resilient to threat. If we can create an Internet of Trusted Data that provides safe, secure access for everyone, then huge societal benefits can be unlocked, including better health, greater financial inclusion, and a population that is more engaged with and better supported by its government.

The future of National Cyber Security should be supported by an Internet of Trusted Data in order to enable both auditable provenance of identity and the credibility of data in order to enhance economic viability of new technology solutions, policies and best practices. Simultaneously, an Internet of Trusted Data must protect the privacy of people, ensure public safety, economic and national security, and foster public, individual and business partnerships.

In order to accomplish these goals thought leaders in federal, state and local governments should join with academia and carrier-scale private industry to work toward an Internet of Trusted Data.

An Internet of Trusted Data includes:

- **Robust Digital Identity**. Identity, whether personal or organizational, is the key that unlocks all other data and data sharing functions. Digital Identity includes not only having unique and unforgeable credentials that work everywhere, but also the ability to access all the data linked to your identity and the ability to control the "persona" that you present in different situations. These pseudonym identities, or personas, include the "work you", the "health system you", the "government you" and many other permutations specific to particular aspects of your individual relationship with another party. Each of these pseudonym identities will have different data access associated with them, and be owned and controlled only by the core "biological you". To accomplish this there needs to be a global strategy for Identity and Access Management that genuinely enables trusted, auditable sharing relationships and functions without compromising personal anonymity or security. Much of the required infrastructure is technically straightforward, the basics were established by the NIST's National Strategy for Trusted Identity in Cyberspace program and now are widely available from, for instance, mobile operators and similar regulated services. The nation now needs to begin requiring such robust digital identity in order to achieve our goals in cybersecurity and universal access.

- **Distributed Internet Trust Authorities**. We have repeatedly seen that centralized system administration is the weakest link in cybersecurity, enabling both insiders and opponents to destroy

our system security with a single exploit.   The most practical
solution to this problem is to have authority distributed among
many trusted actors, so that compromise of one or even a few
authorities does not destroy the system security consensus.
This already standard practice for the highest security systems: no
one single actor can launch nuclear missiles, for instance.   Now
we need to implement this sort of consensus security widely.
Examples such as the blockchain that underlies most digital
cryptocurrencies show that distributed ledgers can provide worldwide security even in very hostile environments. Today there
is a huge amount of investment by private companies to deploy
software defined network technology which can transparently
expose efficient, convenient versions of this consensus ledger
technology, and the U.S. should set policies that take advantage
of these new capabilities in collaboration with the private and
education sectors, in such a way that digital identities can be
originated by individuals and issued with verification from multiple
access providers.

- **Distributed safe computation**. Our critical systems will suffer
  increasing rates of damage and compromise unless we move
  decisively toward pervasive use of data minimization, more
  encryption and distributed computation. Current firewall, event
  sharing, and attack detection approaches are simply not feasible
  as long-run solutions for cybersecurity, and we need to adopt an
  inherently more robust approach.   The "optimal" technology for
  such an inherently safe data ecosystem is currently being built and
  tested, for reference see MIT's ENIGMA project. Because of the
  importance of acting quickly, the EU data protection authorities
  are supporting a simplified, easy-to-deploy version called OPAL

(*Open Algorithms*, which originated at MIT with French support) for pilot testing within certain countries. The concept of OPAL is that instead of copying or sharing data, algorithms are sent to existing databases, executed behind existing firewalls, and only the encrypted results are shared. This minimizes opportunities to attack databases or divert data for unapproved use, but places restrictions on the ability of an ecosystem to collaborate on data when it is in an encrypted state. Note that OPAL may be combined with anonymization identifying elements in order to reduce risk, and in the long run will evolve toward a fully-encrypted, computation friendly model. Approaches such as homomorphic encryption and secure multiparty computation can enable encrypted data to be used in approved, auditable manner by parties that can't decrypt it or read it. In particular, the ability to permissibly ask questions of data in the form of "attributes" will be a key pattern to maintaining digital privacy while enabling innovation ecosystems. The U.S. Government should create a roadmap for progressing from the current situation, through transition technologies such as OPAL, to complete solutions such as MIT ENIGMA. More on OPAL/ENIGMA can be found in Chapter 3.

- **Universal Access**. The advantages of secure digital infrastructure are diminished without universal access. The U.S. Government can promote universal access by policies that provide for secure, citizen-controlled Personal Data Stores for all citizens in a manner analogous to current physical Post Office Boxes, and promote their use by making government benefits and interactions such as tax transfers and information inquiries conveniently available by mobile devices and web interfaces secured by the citizens' digital identity.   Planning by the U.S.

Post Office for such universal Personal Data Stores (Digital Mailboxes) has long been in place, and the secure digital identity infrastructure is already offered by mobile operators and other regulated services.

- **Investment required.** We recommend that the U.S. Government establish a "Living Lab" to not just test, but actually create a small-scale deployment of this new ecosystem under real-world conditions with all available and necessary technology in order to obtain citizen and stakeholder feedback. A Living Lab would prove concept and build citizen confidence towards large scale deployment and prove viability of technical solutions.   We also recommend that the U.S. Government support "microdegrees" leveraging distance education methods (e.g., MOOC, etc.) in order to upgrade the cybersecurity training of the existing workforce. Such continuing education methods have proven quite cost-effective in changing the technology culture within U.S. companies.

The Living Lab provides a venue where researchers and developers can begin to address challenges around the Internet of Trusted Data, providing them with real-world conditions under which a robust identity system must be deployable with distributed trust authorities, as exemplified by proposals to use blockchain technology. It also permits data sharing to be explored at scale while preserving privacy, where algorithms are sent to existing data repositories based on distributed safe computation. Key to the Living Lab is universal access to the benefits of the convergence of these new solutions. Detail on Living Labs is provided in Chapter 7.

INTRODUCTION

Our economies and societies are going through a historical transition from the industrial age of the past two centuries, whose models have been mostly based on physical interactions, to an increasingly digital age based on global, digital interactions. Previous methods for managing identity and data security have proved inadequate in our emerging digital world, and have led to serious cybersecurity breaches.

A number of failure modes emerge at the current transition point.

- While economy and society are becoming digital, identity remains rooted in analog concepts. The consequences of issues such as identity theft include massive fraud, ranging from bank and insurance to tax and even Uber and AirBnb. A parallel issue emerges of equity and fairness: robust digital identities must be available to all individuals.

- Commercial and government organizations have traditionally built silos of IT systems and data stores each are largely incompatible with each other. In order to move to the next level of a digital economy and to attain the speed and efficiency of business moving at the speed of the network, there must be interoperability and sharing to foster public, private and individual collaboration on trusted data. It must be efficient and based on universally agreed protocols while maintaining security and auditability.

At the same time, our increasingly digital world is opening up opportunities for economic inclusion, improved health care, better financial support and populations that are more engaged with and supported by their government.

To help address these threats and opportunities, President Obama issued an Executive Order earlier this year establishing the Commission on Enhancing National Cybersecurity within the Department of Commerce. The Commission was charged with "recommending bold, actionable steps that the government, private sector, and the nation as a whole can take to bolster cybersecurity in today's digital world, and reporting back by the beginning of December."

The Commission invited select members of this working group to participate in a panel on research and development opportunities at a public meeting held in New York City on May 16, 2016. In our testimony to the Commission we highlighted six key areas where government, technology companies and academia should work together in order to increase the speed and quality of the two-way information flows that are essential for developing a data-rich society with a holistic approach to cyber protection:

- **Proof of identity**. A new identity management system must be created to replace today's ad hoc systems.

- **Trustworthy, auditable data provenance.** Systems must automatically track every change that is made to data, so it is auditable and completely trustworthy.

- **Secure, privacy-preserving processing.** We have to enable the entities to engage in transactions and to verify that contracts are being fulfilled but without revealing private or confidential information.

- **Universal access.** Everyone must be able to share in the benefits, and have the protections, of this new trusted data infrastructure

- **Research and development.** We need to dramatically increase the speed and scale of cyber innovation in both the private and public sector by use of "living lab" field trials

- **Workforce development.** Companies face a serious shortage of cyber trained personnel and of management expertise in cybersecurity. We need to increase and maintain the available workforce, which may require greater educational capacity and incentives.

We also emphasized that the essential importance of focusing on complete systems, rather than individual technologies or technology layers, and that they be developed and proven in "living laboratories" with a representative population of users in order to provide feedback about the relevance, efficiency, effectiveness, and ethical dimensions of these new systems.

In discussions with the U.S. Secretary of Commerce, the White House panel on cybersecurity, and the E.U. VP of Single Digital Market, we were encouraged to create a plan for accomplishing these goals that brought together key players from government, industry, and academia.

On July 11, 2016 we convened a workshop at MIT to start framing our statement of the problem as well as our recommendations.
The workshop participants all agreed that we are at a unique point to move forward, much as was the case with the Internet and World Wide Web in the early 1990. As was the case then, there is a growing consensus on:

1.   The problems to be solved:
   - The need to bolster cybersecurity in our increasingly digital economy and society
   - A requirement for universal, highly secure digital identities covering individuals, private and public institutions and "things" (IoT).
   - The need to efficiently access, exchange and share critical data with full security and privacy protection.
   - The overall systems have to be "fault tolerant" in the presence of "non-trusted" actors, whether they are competitors or other governments you only want to share limited data with, or "bad actors" with malicious intent.

2.   The fact that there is promising evolution of a new set of general technologies and potential solutions to help address these problems, including:
   - Identity, whether personal or organizational, and, moreover, the ability to own and assert identity attributes is a lynchpin concern. There needs to be a kind of "internet of identity" to genuinely enable all other sharing functions.
   - Blockchain networks can provide a single source of auditable truth between organizations and some level of appropriate automation of data processing. However, organizations must

decide also on distributed sources of trust for the moderation of such networks. Identity plays a crucial role in enabling blockchain technology to be adopted broadly.

- Overlaying inventions such as personal data stores and secure multiparty computation (see for reference implementations MIT OpenPDS and MIT ENIGMA), we can develop a new digital ecosystem that is secure, trusted, and empowering.

3. The need for the private sector, government and academia to work together to address these critical problems and leverage these promising technologies to enable and incentivize collaboration and innovation.

At the same time, the population needs to be educated in a coherent fashion about the benefits and role that each individual can play in forming this new system.

While the question arises "are we simply replacing known risks with unknown risks?", the shortcomings of existing systems are proving so great that a new approach is needed.

In light of these concerns, we have articulated potential solutions around Robust Identity and Trusted Data which enable the auditability and credibility of both while supporting Fair Information Practice Principles.

THE PROMISE OF ROBUST IDENTITY:

Our mission in suggesting a robust identity framework focuses on connecting the individual with the digital identity, while protecting privacy. When we say "robust", we mean both reliable and non-forgeable.

Benefits include better access:

- to the financial system for the underbanked and unbanked;
- to the health care system, in a fashion that reduces medical error and improves care;
- to government services;
- to other basic services (e.g., making it easier to obtain an apartment or home).

Drivers of need

A number of problems are driving the need for a robust identity:

- It is fundamental to cybersecurity. Current cybersecurity systems are insufficient to the task, as evidenced by the numerous large-scale data breaches recently experienced by both the private and public sectors globally.
- We all need identity to access services.
- The flaws in translating from a physical proof of identity ("I see you in front of me, I know you are you"), to a digital format ("On the internet, no one knows you are a dog"), in a robust and portable fashion.
- The question of authority: who provides the identity?
- The need for it to be unique, strong, verifiable, and non-forgeable.

A potential solution

A new paradigm asserts that you are your digital footprint, and you have ownership rights in your data. Just as the Magna Carta established a framework for individual property rights in 1215 A.D., so too a new digital social contract needs to provide for digital ownership rights.

The concept of behavioral biometrics is gaining ground in areas such as financial services and digital authentication. Research conducted at MIT and elsewhere has demonstrated that behavior biometrics are much more difficult to fabricate and deliver 10X+ better security than password-based models. With respect to ownership rights: this "New Deal on Data" was first posed by us in collaboration with the World Economic Forum in 2009 and expanded since.

Several challenges need to be addressed, including, but not limited to:

- **"Big Brother":** the fear of a government using panoptic access for dictatorship;

- **Bad actors:** whether inside an organization or external, accumulating such data creates risk of misuse by bad actors;

- **Scale and implementation cost:** implementing such a solution globally will have nontrivial scaling and cost functions (and relatedly, who will pay for it and how?);

- **Undocumented residents:** deploying such a system creates potential for institutionalizing a digital divide between rich and poor, and introduces new questions around circumstances such as where municipalities offer undocumented residents a means of identification even if the Federal government hasn't;

- **Equal protection under the law:** how can we protect someone that the system doesn't acknowledge has an existence?

- **Universal vs. silo'd data:** universal data has greater utility, but is generally less secure – siloing can provide a measure of security, but raises issues of interoperability; and

- **Regulatory lag:** there is always a gap between a technology innovation and the ability of policymakers and regulators to implement an appropriate framework around it.

Questions also remain as to how this would be developed. Should it be government led, like the EID or India or Estonia? Should it be furnished by industry, similar to how Internet Domain Name registries are handled? Should it be housed within a nonprofit or academic environment, like the Kerberos Consortium or the World Wide Web Consortium (W3C)? Active dialog with key stakeholders is required to establish the optimal path.

Potential Solution: Core Identities and Persona Identities

At the heart of digital identities is the concept of the core identity of an individual, which inalienably belongs to that individual. The core identity serves as the quantum from which emerge other forms of digitally-derived identities (called personas), that are practically useful and are legally enforced in digital transactions. An individual must have the freedom to choose to deploy one or more digital personas on the Internet, each used with specific sharing and access permission and tailored to the specific aspect of that individual's life. Each digital personal would carry varying degrees of legal enforceability as relevant to the auditable usage context of that persona.

The individual must be able to use transaction-identities derived from his or her relevant persona, without affecting the privacy of their core identity. This derivation process must also allow the relying party (counterparty) in a transaction to validate the source-authenticity and strength of provenance of the transaction identity, without affecting the privacy of the core identity of the user. New cryptographic techniques – such as zero knowledge proofs – offer a promising direction in providing solutions for privacy-preserving core identities.

As currently configured, existing business models, legal instruments and technical implementations are insufficient to support this type of identity ecosystem. This is because something is missing: an architecture for individual ownership of and primacy over one's own core identity and which entities or relationships have access to attributes of that identity. With such a core identity, it is possible for multiple aliases, accounts and attributes to be authenticated and authorized in a reliable, privacy enhancing and scalable manner. To this end, a viable identity infrastructure provides a way for each person to own their single underlying core identity and to bind several "personas" to that core identity without the need for other parties to access the core identity or be aware of any other personas. With this approach, government issued identity credentials such as driver licenses, passports, professional licenses, birth certificates, etc.) as well as strong-provenanced sources of attributes about a person (e.g. banks for credit scores, etc) can be leveraged to create a core identity that remains private to the end-user.

A key feature of the new model is that it must allow entities in the ecosystem to (i) verify the "quality" or security of an identity, and (ii) to assess the relative "freedom" or independence of an identity from any given authority (e.g. government, businesses, etc.), and (iii) to assess the source of trust for a digital identity.

We believe a new model for digital identities for future blockchain systems is required, which is summarized in the following progressive steps:

1. **Strong provenanced attributes:** It must be founded on an existing real-world identity which has a high degree of source of trust, where its attributes have a high degree of provenance. This identity maybe issued by an existing identity provider or other trusted third party operating within a legal jurisdiction (e.g. Bank, Government, Service Provider, etc.).

2. **Transitive source of trust:** Create a "Core Identity" based on the existing high quality identity. That is, use a privacy-preserving algorithm that translates the existing real-world identity with strong provenance into a digital core-identity which carries-over the source of trust.

3. **Self-issued derived identities as personas:** Provide users with the freedom (and algorithms/tools) to establish personas and to self-issue anonymous but verifiable transaction-identities, each of which is cryptographically derived from the user's core-identity and each of which carries specific permissioned attributes suitable for the purpose of the transaction-identities. The source of trust from the core-identity must also be carried-over into the derived transaction-identity.

4.   **Privacy-preserving verification:** Provide the Relying Parties (counter-party) with privacy-preserving verification algorithms to validate the source of trust for any given (anonymous) transaction-identity. These verification algorithms must allow a relying party to establish a chain of provenance (from the transaction-identity all the way back to the origin attributes and core-identity), while preserving the privacy of the owner of the identity.

5.   **Legal Trust Framework (LTF):** Establish an identity ecosystem for blockchain based on a LTF for core-identities, personas and anonymous but verifiable transaction-identities. Such a legal framework is already in use for identity-federation schemes in the industry today, and may be used as the legal basis for this new model.

A legal trust framework is a certification program that enables a party who accepts a digital identity credential (called the relying party) to trust the identity, security, and privacy policies of the party who issues the credential (called the identity service provider) and vice versa. An LTF applies within a given deployment ecosystem, such as identity-federation or across two partner organizations.

We believe the current LTFs as practiced in the industry can be extended for usage in blockchain systems. New types of entities will be needed specifically for blockchain ecosystems. We denote these as the *Core-Identity Provider* and *Transaction-Identity Providers* which extends the current role of the Identity Provider (IdP).

The Core-Identity Provider takes a user's existing identity which has a high degree of source of trust and converts it using a privacy-preserving function into a private or secret core identity that is maintained as private or secret, and is only supplied to the Transaction-Identity Provider. The latter then provides a transaction-identity issuance service to the user, as well as a validation service to the relying parties. The user is free to obtain one or more anonymous transaction-identities from the Transaction-Identity Provider or self-issue a derived transaction-identity, all the while maintaining their privacy. The transaction-identities can be used on the blockchain system with other users (relying parties) or on the Internet. The validation service offered by the Transaction-Identity Provider allows a relying-party to inquire about the status and source-grade of a given anonymous transaction-identity prior to transacting.

In the context of blockchains, the LTF provides the following:

- **Network scalability:** It allows any two parties to transact on a blockchain without prior engagement, thus achieving network scalability.

- **Provenance assessment:** It allows a relying-party (counter-party) to assess the "trustworthiness" (provenance and quality) of an (anonymous) transaction-identity prior to commencing the transaction;

- **Cross-jurisdiction interoperability:** It provides a legal foundation for core-identities and (anonymous) transaction-identities to be recognized in differing legal jurisdictions;

- **New business models:** It incentivizes service-providers (including the Core-Identity Providers and Transaction-identity Providers) to develop new business models around new scalable services and permissible use of attribute data associated with identities;

- **Risk assessment and risk management:** It provides entities in the ecosystem with a means of assessing risk and of legal recourse in unforeseen circumstances (e.g. attacks to the service; identity leaks; identity-data theft, provider negligence, etc.) as specified in the LTF operational contracts.

DATA SHARING

Data is rapidly proliferating from an end-user perspective, without a good solution to manage user data as well as identities efficiently. We need a new paradigm for data sharing that preserves user privacy, while allowing data to be shared more globally for the benefit of society.

The constituents served by this new system include both enterprises and average consumers. By bringing control back to the consumer, both data and identity, we can drive better outcomes. We can create technology that would enable the simplification and securing of digital identities through simpler "form factors."

Questions remain – what exactly does this solution look like? Could it be like Global Entry? Who would manage such a system? In Global Entry's case, it's the TSA.

With respect to R&D, there's a great diversity of work required, which we need to approach, as outlined in Section V. Opportunities created from this solution include the creation of digital marketplace for personal data, that would simultaneously provide assurance of your data.

Key Concepts in a Potential Solution

Data sharing in a privacy preserving manner requires a new view on data. There are a number of key concepts and design principles that need to be addressed through an evolutionary proof-of-concept (PoC) implementation. Some of these key concepts are as follows:

1. **Moving the algorithm to the data:** The concept here is to perform the algorithm (i.e. query) execution at the location of data (referred to as the data-repository). This implies that raw-data should never leave its repository, and access to it is controlled by the repository/data owner.

2. **Open Algorithms:** Algorithms (i.e. queries or scripts) must be openly published, studied and vetted by experts to be "safe" from violating the privacy requirements and other requirements stemming from the context of their use.

3. **Permissible Use:** When performing computation on attributes or data associated with identities, respect the explicit and implicit permission, or consent, given for use of the data or identity attributes as part of the transaction.

4.   **Always return "safe answers" (never raw data):** When performing computation (e.g. in answering a query), the data-repository must always return "safe answers" and never raw data. This concept seeks to address the issue of data privacy and the potential danger of de-identification (of Personally Identifying Information, or PII) through the correlation of multiple responses.

5   **Data always in encrypted state:** Data should be encrypted at all times, namely at-rest, in-transit and during computation. Data should not need to be decrypted prior to computation and then re-encrypted afterwards. Advanced cryptographic techniques are now emerging that allows limited forms of computations to be performed on the encrypted data.

There are two broad scenarios we seek to address:

- **Computation by individual repository:** Here, computation over encrypted data is performed by a single repository, which may employ a physically distributed set of nodes (e.g. P2P collaboration network) to collaboratively store parts of the data for increased resiliency against attacks. Cryptographic techniques such as secret-sharing schemes provides for interesting possibilities in addressing these requirements.

- **Collaborative computation by multiple parties (multiparty computation):** Some form of queries may require answers to be computed by multiple participants (e.g. repositories) in a collaborative/quorum method whilst maintaining the privacy of data stored at each repository. Each participant may see the final group-computed value, but they must not see each other's raw data. Cryptographic techniques such as Multi-Party Computation (MPC) offer a path forward in solving these scenarios.

6. **Networked Collaboration Environments and Blockchains for audit and accountability:** Peer-to-Peer (P2P) networks – such as those underlying the Hyperledger system – offers an attractive solution for data resiliency and scalability specially when combined with cryptographic techniques such as secret-sharing and MPC. The consensus-based ledger mechanism underlying these blockchain systems offers a way to perform logging, audit and accounting of queries executed against data in distributed repositories.

7 **Social and economic incentives:** For privacy-preserving data, sharing to scale and being adopted by a wide range of stakeholders, social and economic incentives must be provided, not only for persons or organizations holding "edge data" but also for infrastructure providers. These infrastructure providers are entities who deliver P2P network scalability, as well as efficient edge computing services that yield real-time edge analytics and visibility into the state of data sharing.

The overall goal of any proposed solution should be increased data protection and privacy, together with scalability, performance and interoperability. In the following, we describe different evolutionary phase of a solution, where each phases focuses on one or more of the above key concepts.

Solution - Phase I "Deployed Blockchain"

The goal here is to explore the use of small number of independent data repositories together with P2P nodes and blockchain technology such as Hyperledger:

- **API-driven query/response controls:** The API defined at the data-repository provides a "hard-wired" query capability. The Querier performs the query by sending a message to the API at the repository, which in turn sends results to the Querier. The API itself defines the type of query accepted, and the granularity of answers being returned.

- **Aggregate answers only:** The API will return "safe answers" in the form of aggregate/statistical answers only. This approach conforms to the key principle of never allowing raw-data to leave the repository.

- **Multiple repositories:** Multiple data-repositories are envisioned where each repository may store only one kind of data (e.g. GPS location) that are constrained through its APIs. To the Querier, the nodes on the Networked Collaboration Environment allows Querier to get access to large number data-repositories – represented as nodes of the P2P network (i.e. nodes on the blockchain).

- **Metadata for discovery:** Sharing of data presumes the existence of data is known. A number of nodes on the Networked Collaboration Environment may take the role of "metadata directories", where they can return information regarding the location of nodes with desired data.

- **All access request/response logged:** Direct capture of logs into a blockchain is inefficient and does not scale well. Instead, approaches such as those in Blue Horizon offer a more promising solution. Each party (the Querier and data repository) tracks the API calls, and then hashes the logs. Each party must generate the same hash for the calls, as well as the same hash for data sent/received. These hashes can be written to the blockchain and can be audited by each party only (for privacy preservation).

- **Authorization and Identity:** Authorization tokens will be used in conjunction with a basic blockchain identity, with the focus primarily on authorizations to access a data-repository through the published APIs. The member services capability of systems such as Hyperledger can begin to be explored in this phase.

Solution - Phase II "Bring Algorithms to the Data"

Building on the previous phase, the goal in this phase is to introduce the use of algorithms or scripts that are vetted to be safe for a given classification of data. These vetted algorithms can be signed and published (e.g. at nodes of the Networked Collaboration Environment). Invocation of one of these published algorithms by a Querier will require all the conditions stated be fulfilled (e.g. identity of the Querier is verified, target data repositories, authorization tokens, etc.). This approach builds on access APIs from the previous phase, with tighter restrictions expressed through vetting of algorithms. The Querier's choice of algorithm can be recorded on the blockchain, with the returned results being logged and recorded on the blockchain. Furthermore, a published algorithm can be expressed as a smart contract residing in one or more of nodes on the Networked Collaboration Environment.

- **Query control using vetted algorithms/scripts:** Queries are expressed as executable "algorithms" or scripts. The Querier sends the algorithm to the relevant end-points located at the data-repositories.

- **Flexible queries:** In this phase the queries have greater flexibility than the API-driven approach in Phase I. Subset SQL or Python may be considered as the query/scripts language.

- **Vetting of safe algorithms:** Algorithms are first vetted by experts for their safety and impact to privacy and to the correctness of returned results. Only aggregate/statistical queries are permitted. Copies of all approved/vetted queries are signed and then stored at a number of nodes on the Networked Collaboration Environment (participating in blockchain) for public verification.

- **Repositories evaluate and execute algorithms:** Each repository must dedicate computational power ("compute engine") to execute/evaluate a received query (in the form of an algorithm) against the available local data. Raw-data itself is never returned.

- **Richer data repositories:** Each repository is assumed to store richer sets of data of varying types.

- **Authorization & Privacy-preserving Identities:** The identity of the Querier and the repositories need to be preserved from "leakages" of information through methods such as correlations and others that disclose private information. Basic transaction identities can be deployed, as part of managing identity, privacy and confidentiality on the network. Some blockchain systems (e.g. Hyperledger) provide a suitable framework for "member services" (i.e. user's core identity and transaction identities).

- **Blockchain used for logs and monitoring:** A blockchain is used to log all access request/responses for audit and post-event traffic analysis.

Solution - Phase III "Basic MPC"

This phase introduces more sophisticated cryptographic techniques that support privacy-preserving distributed computations over data,once such technique is a secure multi-party computation (S-MPC). Here an SMPC cryptographic algorithm is used for computation over data that is stored in plaintext at the repository. A select number of nodes on the blockchain have SMPC capability, and can participate in Secure MPC computation instances. Focus is on the performance aspects of a small number of MPC-nodes, including computational performance and network bandwidth measurements. An MPC-node may be implemented as an "overlay" over nodes in a blockchain system. A rudimentary proof-of-MPC-completion may be recorded on the underlying blockchain.

- **Raw data remains locally at the repositories:** The data remains private, and none of the nodes see each other's raw data. Furthermore, each data-item is located at its "home" data repository (i.e. not at a P2P set of nodes).

- **Data at rest in plaintext (not encrypted):** Data-at-rest, a given repository is in plaintext and not hidden using secret-sharing encryption. This allows focus to be directed to MPC algorithms and their performance.

- **Simple MPC configuration of known nodes:** A small number of repositories (e.g. 3 nodes) can be used to create a group of parties involved in the MPC computation. Each node in an MPC instance will employ a secure channel (e.g. TLS1.2) to ensure integrity protection from attacks, and each know the others identity (e.g. via X509 certificates).

- **Predefined simple queries:** Only simple queries will be addressed, possibly as pre-defined (template) queries. Complex queries (e.g. inner/outer joins of tables) will be left for future work.

- **Metadata service:** Types of data and available simple operations are "advertised" at a special server, to which Queries can locate relevant repositories.

- **Rudimentary Proof-of-MPC-Completion:** MPC-nodes need to record the completion of their MPC-computation on the underlying blockchain, with a matching verification/validation mechanism. The proof is to be determined, but may consist of each MPC-node listing its steps and message flows (with other MPC-nodes), and recording these on the blockchain for later replay/verification. This aspect is relevant for providing economic incentive nodes to participate within a given MPC computation.

Solution - Phase IV "Full MPC with Secret Sharing"

This phase employs a combination of two sophisticated cryptographic techniques, namely the Secure MPC technique (from the previous phase) together with data encrypted into pieces (or "shares"). A minimal "threshold" number of shares are required to re-construct the original data item. A select number of nodes on the blockchain store "shares" of a data item but never the complete set of shares, providing resiliency against attacks seeking to recover the data item. These are called "Shares-node". The MPC-nodes are now also responsible for collecting the relevant shares of each data item from the underlying Shares-nodes in the blockchain. Each Share-node may hold shares corresponding to different data-items, which in turn belong to different owners. The Querier sends the algorithm/query to a coordinating-node that represents the Querier to the MPC-nodes.

- **No centralized data-repository:** Data-repositories no longer hold any complete data, but only location of other nodes (shares-nodes) in the decentralized Networked Collaboration Environment that hold data (in the form of encrypted data-shares). As the "owner" of a data-item, the data-repository must perform shares management (i.e. shares creation, distribution and re-locations).

- **Shares distribution, re-collection and management:** Each data-repository implements a "standardized" shares location-management function that support the creation of shares-coordinates (of all the relevant shares for each data item). The shares-coordinates are then given to the designated MPC-node involved in a given query instance.

- **MPC only nodes:** A new category of nodes will be introduced whose purpose is to participate in and complete an MPC computation instance. This distinction allows for support of an "outsourcing" model whereby the data repository (who now holds no actual data) delegates the MPC computation instance to a given MPC-node.

- **Shares-based primitive operations:** Simple operations (additions and multiplications) over the encrypted-shares.

- **Query-to-primitive translation:** Simple translator from subset SQL into the relevant MPC primitives (additions and operations).

- **Authorization for invoking MPC-nodes:** The Querier must provide authorization evidence that it authorized to request the set of MPC-nodes to collect corresponding shares and to perform MPC computation on these shares.

INVESTMENT REQUIRED

R&D investment is needed to implement the solutions suggested herein. In evaluating an R&D plan, what can we leverage that already exists out there, and what would we need to build.

We recommend that the U.S. Government establish a "Living Lab" to not just test, but actually deploy, this new paradigm. A Living Lab would prove concept and build confidence towards a national and international rollout. MIT has employed the Living Lab model in communities as diverse as Hamburg in Germany, the country of Senegal, and Cambridge MA.

We would envision a test starting with 10,000 people, then 100,000+,
then 1+ million (roughly logarithmic proof of concept scaling). It could
begin with a neighborhood or small community, then a town or larger
neighborhood, then a midsize city. It could be deployed to a specific
department within the Federal Government. Or, it could be structured
on an interest group or common problem area ("affinity-driven"), such
as veterans or federal workers.

Competitions such as the Department of Transportation Smart City
Challenge, with a $50 million prize for the winning proposal, illustrate
a viable model for generating a diverse set of perspectives on the
problem and potential solutions.

Criteria for Site Selection
1.   Town-scale
2.   Proximity to a substantial federal facility
3.   End points: consumers, health system, financial system
4.   Make interoperable with things that are not new?
5.   Advisable: strong local university partner
6.   Coordinating "owner" locally

Geographies that meet these characteristics include Boulder CO,
Austin TX, Rochester NY, Hartford CT, and Boston MA. Affinity-driven
examples include the Veterans Administration or the USPS. A federally
administered competition could stimulate innovation much in the
same way that the ARPANet and NSFnet led to the development of the
commercial internet.

Background

The Massachusetts Institute of Technology Connection Science initiative (MIT Connection Science) hosted a working group session on 11 July 2016 in Cambridge, MA to answer the call posed by the White House Commission on Cybersecurity, and separate discussions among and bewteen Professor Pentland and the U.S. Secretary of Commerce Penny Pritzker and the European Union's Vice President Ansip, in charge of the Single Digital Market. This document reflects a distillation of the discussion from the July 11 working group.

Participating were:
- Alex Pentland (Professor, MIT)
- Irving Wladawsky-Berger (MIT Connection Science Fellow)
- David Shrier (Managing Director, MIT Connection Science)
- Jerry Cuomo (IBM Fellow and Vice President Blockchain Technologies)
- Steve Davis (Senior Consultant, Payments Innovation, MasterCard)
- Michael Frank (Program Director, Blockchain Technologies, IBM)
- Thomas Hardjono (Chief Technology Officer, MIT Connection Science)
- Guerney Hunt (Research Staff Member, IBM)
- Cameron Kerry (Visiting Scholar, MIT; Distinguished Visiting Fellow, Brookings Institution; formerly General Counsel and Acting Secretary, U.S. Dept. of Commerce)
- Mark O'Riley (Office of the General Counsel, Government and Regulatory Affair- Technology Policy, IBM)
- Chris Parsons (Vice President Big Data Strategy and Business Development, AT&T)
- Gari Singh (Distinguished Engineer & Blockchain CTO, IBM)
- Anne Shere Wallwork (Senior Counselor for Strategic Policy, Office of Terrorist Financing and Financial Crimes, U.S. Department of the Treasury)
- Rod Walton (VP Qualcomm)
- Irida Xheneti (Entrepreneur in Residence, MIT Connection Science)

CHAPTER 2

Core ID:
Core Identities for Future
Transaction Systems

Thomas Hardjono, David Shrier and Alex Pentland

Blockchain technology as a paradigm for a decentralized and immutable shared ledger promises new and interesting development for the future Internet. The rise into prominence of blockchain technology has also rekindled interest in the notion of an identity ecosystem that is not only scalable (beyond the blockchain) but also preserves the privacy of individuals and organizations that transact on the shared ledger.

The call for an identity ecosystem that is privacy-preserving and scalable is also echoed in the recent NSTIC whitepaper[1] on the *National Strategy for Trusted Identities in Cyberspace*. Specifically, the NSTIC strategy document calls for an identity ecosystem that will minimize the ability to link credential use among multiple service providers, thereby preventing them from developing a complete picture of an individual's activities online. This sentiment is also echoed elsewhere[2,3,4,5,6].

Today there are a number of unsolved challenges with regards to digital identities for the Internet and for blockchain systems:

- **Identity tied to services:** Most digital identities (commonly understood today as email addresses) are created as an adjunct construction to support access to services provided on the Internet. This tight coupling between digital identity and service providers has given rise to the unmanageable proliferation of user-accounts and credential on the Internet. Users today are still asked to create an account and identity each time they access a new service on the Internet.

- **Privacy of transaction identities:** A major shortcoming in current identity systems on the Internet is the lack of privacy with respect to transactions performed using these identities. The existing Bitcoin-blockchain as well as new blockchain systems, smart contracts and shared ledgers (e.g. Ethereum[19]; Corda[20]) may suffer from similar shortcomings of identity on the Internet, namely that of disclosing personally identifying information (PII) over time, either directly or via "leakage" through the sheer number of transactions. Our previous research[21,22,23,24] has indicated that even a small number of transactions can reveal PII information.

- **Massive duplication of personal data across the Internet:** Together with the proliferation of user-accounts comes the massive duplication of personal data across numerous service providers on the Internet. These service providers are essentially holding the same set of personal data or attributes belonging to a user or consumer (e.g. name, address, phone, credit card, etc.).

- **Increased risk of attacks and increased liability:** Service providers and organizations that hold personal data are increasingly subject to attacks – external as well as internal – that are costly to business. New regulations, such as the GDPR in Europe[2,3,4] increase the legal liability of these service providers in the face of data breaches and identity theft.

- **Inefficient business model:** The current forms of identities (as simple email addresses and cookies) are designed for and operate based on a business model that seeks to understand and harness consumer social behavior, but which relies on inaccurate data. Rather than creating siloes of personal data, businesses and identity providers need to share user data in a privacy-preserving manner. Sharing of data increases its value, especially when data is shared across domains or verticals[7].

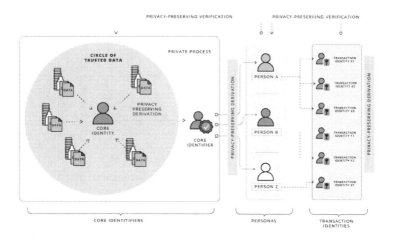

Figure 1: Core Identities, Personas and Transaction Identities for a User

In this paper we argue that a scalable identity ecosystem must be developed on a coherent paradigm for privacy-preserving data sharing, because the ability to create strongly-provenanced digital identities depends on the extent to which personal data can be shared in a privacy-preserving manner. We argue that approaches such as MIT OPAL/ENIGMA [8,9] for privacy-preserving data sharing offers a better foundation for future internet identities based on information about a user, which has stronger provenance compared to "shallow" user information that is in possession today, of most identity providers.

Furthermore, we argue that certain types of identities – referred to as *core identities* – are inherently private or secret to the individual possessing it and to the entities that "sign" the core identity by providing transaction or other personal data[10,11]. For example, part of the core identity may be co-created by a bank that manages an individual's bank account and asserts that the individual has a valid bank account. Core identities should be the foundation for *persona* identities that represent a narrow "slice" of a person's life. Thus, a person will have multiple persona identities created for each of their work, social, family or other communities within which they belong.

We believe that data (personal data) needs to be viewed differently from digital identity, and that a useful digital identity must be derived from data with strong provenance. For privacy-preservation, we also advocate that operationally strong-provenance data needs to be separated from the derived digital identities. Today, an example of this separation of data from digital identity can be found in the card payment industry where a merchant does not need to know personal data about the cardholder in order to process a credit-card transaction. Personal data about the cardholder is held by the Issuing Bank and related organizations. Furthermore, the loss of a credit-card number does not result in the loss of the consumer's personal data.

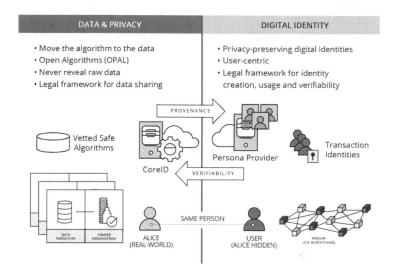

DATA & PRIVACY	DIGITAL IDENTITY
• Move the algorithm to the data • Open Algorithms (OPAL) • Never reveal raw data • Legal framework for data sharing	• Privacy-preserving digital identities • User-centric • Legal framework for identity creation, usage and verifiability

CORE IDENTITIES: KEY CONCEPTS

There are a number of key concepts and principles underlying the notion of core identities, core identifiers and personas (see Figure 1). In the following we discuss these in the context of personal data and digital identities on the Internet.

A fundamental concept in our proposal is that of *derived identities and identifiers*[10] which provides not only privacy to its user (the person or organization that it represents) but also a degree of defense in the case of attacks against identity providers (e.g. identity theft) and for a safety net in the rare case of weaknesses within the underlying cryptographic implementations.

We argue that *transaction identities and identifiers* are the forms of identities that should be used on the Internet and that they must be derived (e.g. cryptographically) from a core identity which itself must be kept as private or secret. Should a transaction identity be compromised or stolen, it can be placed on a public "blacklist" and a new one be derived for the user. The derivation process or algorithms must maintain the privacy of the user and the secrecy of the user's core identity.

We define identity* as *the collective aspect* of the set of characteristic or features by which a thing (e.g. human; device; organization) is recognizable and distinguishable one from another. In the context of a human person, *individuality* of a person plays an important role in that it allows a community of people to recognize the distinct characteristics of an individual person and consider the person as a persisting entity.

- **Core identity:** The collective aspect of the set of characteristics (as represented by personal data) by which a person is uniquely recognizable, and from which a unique *core identifier* may be generated based on the set of relevant personal data[10,11]. Thus, for example, the set of transaction data associated with a person can be collated and be used to create a core identity that distinguishes that person from others. Out of this set of transaction data, a core identifier may be generated and be held as a joint secret by its issuer and the person. The core identity pertaining to a person must be kept secret, and not be used in transactions.

---

* Etymology: Middle French identité, from Late Latin identitat-, identitas, probably from Latin identidem repeatedly, contraction of idem et idem, literally, same and same (Merriam-Webster Dictionary).

- **Core Identifier:** A secret data (e.g. string) or secret mechanism (e.g. crypto function) that uniquely identifies a person or entity. The core identifier must be immutable, must be kept secret, and never be used directly in transactions.

- **Persona:** A persona is defined by and created based on a collection of attributes used in a given context or a given relationship. Thus, a person may have a work-persona, home-persona, social-persona, and others. Each of these personas is context-dependent and involves only the relevant subset of the core identity characteristics of that person. A person may have one or more personas.

- **Transaction Identity and Identifier:** When an individual seeks to perform a transaction (e.g. on the Internet, on a blockchain or other transacting mediums) he or she chooses a relevant persona and derives from that persona *a transaction identity* (and corresponding digital identifier) to be used in the transaction. A transaction identity maybe short-lived and may even be created only for that single transaction instance. A useful analogy is that of credit card numbers, which may be used at a Point of Sale (POS) locations without the user needing to provide any additional identifiers (i.e. reveal data from their core identity such as Social Security Number) and which may be replaced at any time without impacting the user's core identity.

TRUSTED DATA: FOUNDATION FOR CORE IDENTITIES

Data with known provenance, quality and accuracy represents a crucial ingredient in the creation of core identities. In the real world economy, multiple entities (e.g. government, organizations, etc.) generate and process data pertaining to individuals[3].

For a given domain or vertical, many of these entities inevitably become authoritative sources of information regarding a person by virtue of handling data regarding that person – either through their need for fulfilling regulatory compliance requirements or through the sheer number of repeated transaction pertaining to the person.

In seeking to address the need for a *personal data sharing ecosystem* – as a foundation of the future digital identity on the Internet – there are a number of considerations that come into play regarding core identities and the personal data upon which it is built:

- **The usefulness of a core identity depends on quality of data:** The quality of data that captures the set of characteristics of a person defines the quality of and therefore usefulness of the core identity created from the data.

- **Sharing of personal data increases accuracy:** Sharing of data regarding a subject increases the accuracy of information that can be asserted regarding the subject or person[6]. Since privacy of the person is paramount in establishing core identities, only appropriately aggregated data should be shared and never raw or individually identifiable data.

- **Open algorithms for sharing personal data:** Use concepts in Open Algorithms (OPAL)[8] when sharing personal data. In sharing personal data for the purpose of establishing core identities, perform the algorithm (i.e. query) execution at the location of data (referred to as the data-repository). Algorithms (i.e. queries or scripts) must be openly published, studied and vetted by experts to be "safe" from violating the privacy requirements and other requirements stemming from the context of their use. When performing computation (e.g. in answering a query), the data-repository must always return "safe answers" and never raw data. This concept seeks to address the issue of data privacy and the potential danger of de-identification (of Personally Identifying Information, or PII) through the correlation of multiple responses.

- **Joint creation of core identities:** Entities that contribute to the construction of a core identity by asserting personal properties of the person (e.g., "they have a bank account with us") are a co-creator of the core identity and subsequent personas derived from the core identity. This includes the personas and transaction identities. When performing computation on attributes or data associated with identities, respect the explicit and implicit permission, or consent, given for use of the data or identity attributes as part of the transaction[8].

- **Core identities must be private and secret:** Just as personal data is private or secret to an individual, a core identity generated from personal data must also be private or secret to the individual and to a small number of entities who contributed in creating the core identity[10,11].

- **Core identities and core identifiers must never be used in transactions:** Since a core identity represents the collective aspect of the set of characteristic that distinguishes a person and therefore is privacy-sensitive, a core identity must never be used directly in a transaction. Instead, one or more personas derived from a core identity must be created, out of which transaction identities can be generated[10].

- **Circles of trust for sharing aggregate data:** Entities or organizations that "sign" the core identity by contributing assertions (e.g., asserting that the individual has an active bank account) should do so under the legal framework of a *Circle of Trust*[†] (CoT) that includes the individual.

- **Legal Trust Framework**: A Circle of Trust for the sharing of aggregated personal data must be codified in the form of a *Legal Trust Framework*[12,13,14,15] that specifies the entities involved in the CoT, the type/kind of personal data used, and the Open Algorithms used for sharing aggregations of personal data. This allows assessment of the quality and legal status of the core identity.

- **Issuer of core identities for the circle of trust:** Each Circle of Trust that seeks to issue core identities (and other downstream derived identities) based on shared aggregated data should establish a *Core Identity Issuer* service that tasked to create and manage core identities in that community.

---

† The notion of the Circle of Trust originated from the Liberty Alliance consortium in early 2000. The Alliance shaped the technology into what is known today as the Security Assertions Markup Language (SAML2.0) [16][17].

A Circle of Trust (CoT) can be formed for various purposes, including for verticals (e.g. banking; insurance), government sectors (e.g. DoD employees), social communities (e.g. town residents) and so on. The primary determinant is whether the CoT has sufficient data regarding a user/member, whether it can provide privacy-preserving access to the data regarding a user and the legal structure underlying the CoT.

CORE IDENTITY ISSUERS

The goal of a *Core Identity Issuer* (CoreID Issuer) is to collate sufficient data – aggregate data and non-PII data -- from members of a given Circle of Trust in order to create a Core Identity and Core Identifier for a given user (See Figure 2). The Issuer performs this task as a trusted member of the Circle of Trust, governed by rules of operations (i.e. legal contract) and with the consent of the user. Architectures and techniques such as MIT OPAL/ENIGMA can be used here in order for the CoreID Issuer to obtain privacy-preserving aggregate data from the various sources who are members of the Circle of Trust.

The goals of the Core-ID Issuer within a Circle of Trust are as follows:

- **Onboard a member-user:** The Issuer's primary function is to on-board users who are known to the CoT community, and who have requested and consented to the creation of a Core Identity.

- **Collate PII-free data into a Core Identity:** The Issuer obtains aggregate data and other PII-free data regarding the user from members of the CoT. This becomes the core identity for the user, which is retained by the Issuer for the duration selected by the user. The Issuer must keep the core identity as secret, accessible only to the user.

- **Generate core identifier (unlinkable):** For a given user and their core identity, the Issuer generates a core identifier (e.g. random number) that must be unlinkable to the core identity. Note that a core identifier must not be used in a transaction.
  The core identifier value may be contained as a signed certificate or other signed data structure, with the Persona Provider as its intended audience (see Figure 2).

- **Issue core assertions regarding the core identifier:**
  The purpose of the Issuer generating a core identifier is to allow PII-free core-assertions regarding the user to be created. These signed core assertions[16,17] must retain the privacy of the user, and must declare assertions about the core identifier.

- *Interface with Persona Providers*: The Issuer's main audience is the Persona Provider, who must operate with the Issuer under legal trust framework that calls-out user privacy as a strict requirement. The Issuer must make available the necessary *issuance end-points* (i.e. APIs) as well as *validation end-points* to the Persona Provider. In some cases, from an operational deployment view the Issuer and Persona Provider may be co-located or even tightly coupled under the same provider entity, although the functional difference and boundaries are clear.

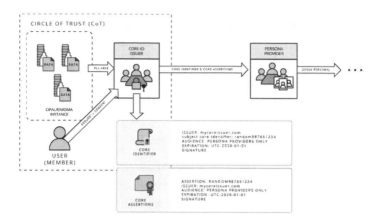

Figure 2: Core Identity Issuer, Core Identifiers and Core Assertions

PERSONA PROVIDERS AND TRANSACTION IDENTITIES

The primary goal of a Persona Provider is to create and manage one or more *persona identities* as a service to the end-user who is a member of a given Circle of Trust. The Persona Provider does not need to be a member of the Circle of Trust, but must rely on the CoreID Issuer upstream for signed assertions regarding the user.

A persona provider differs from the current (traditional) Identity Providers and PKI Service Providers in the following ways:

- **Extension of CoreID Issuer:** The Persona Provider acts as an extension of the CoreID Issuer, by interfacing with other digital entities on the Internet through identity-related services. Relying Parties (Counterparty) and other entities engage with the Persona Provider and never with the CoreID Issuer.

- **Create and maintain personas on behalf of users:** A user creates a persona account (similar to current email accounts) at the Persona Provider by using his or her Core Identifier and Core Assertions. The user never submits personal information to the Persona Provider. The Persona Provider can at any time verify the validity of any Core Identifier and Core Assertions to the CoreID-Issuer.

- **Generate privacy-preserving transaction identities:** A fundamental function of a Persona Provider is to generate one or more transaction identities which are derived (e.g. cryptographically) from the user's core identifier (See Figure 3). These transaction identities must be such that they are "provably derived" from the user's core identifier but with the proving process or algorithm maintaining the privacy of the core identifier. Cryptographic methods such as zero-knowledge proofs[25] (ZKP) protocols offer a promising direction for anonymous but verifiable transaction identities (see, for example,[26,27,28,29,30,31,34]).

- **Validation service:** Similar to validation services in the PKI space, a Persona Provider also makes available a validation service endpoint to which relying parties (counterparty) can query the status of a given transaction-identity that was issued by the Persona Provider.

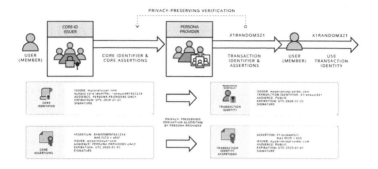

Figure 3: Deriving Transaction Identities

The Persona Provider never sees any private data regarding the user, and ideally the user is anonymous (or semi-anonymous) to the Persona Provider. The Persona Provider consumes the core identifier and core assertions from the CoreID Issuer (which are intended for the Persona Provider), and issues one or more Persona Identities (e.g. "Joe at Work", "Joe at Home", "Joe at Golf Club", etc). For each persona, one or more anonymous (or semi-anonymous) but verifiable transaction-identities are created.

When the User engages a Counterparty (Relying Party) in a transaction, the User employs one of the anonymous-verifiable transaction-identities with the relevant assertions (see Figure 4). The Counterparty uses its own persona provider to request the verification of the received transaction-identity and assertions. The Counterparty's persona provider has the option to request validation to the original persona provider (the User's persona provider) who maintains a persona account for the User and who issued the transaction-identity and assertions.

It is worthwhile noting that the interactions shown in Figure 4 are not something new, but has instead existed in the credit card industry for over three decades. In this *Four-Corners Model* an Issuer bank (persona provider) creates a new credit card number of the User who employs it to make purchases at a Merchant (the Counterparty). The Merchant queries a Merchant Acquirer Bank or payments gateway the Counterparty's persona provider regarding the status of the User's credit card.

What differentiates the transaction flows in Figure 4 from the traditional banking Four Corners Model is the use of anonymous but verifiable transaction-identities. Furthermore, depending on the precise model of zero-knowledge proofs used to implement the flows, the User may even be anonymous from the point of view of the Counterparty's Persona Provider – in which case identity validation may require the participation of the User in the zero knowledge proofs protocol[29,30,31].

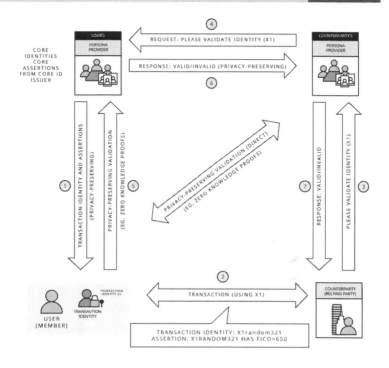

Figure 4: Transaction Identities: Four Corners Model
and the role of Zero Knowledge Proofs

PRIVACY AND KYC: CHAIN OF VERIFIABILITY

The recent rise of Bitcoin[18] and its use of self-asserted public-key pairs
have rekindled interest in the use schemes such as PGP[35] for digital
identities where a self-generated public key is used as a means of
identification. These approaches, however, ignore the reality that for
a transaction to be successful, the relying party (counterparty) must
not only accept the form of identity (e.g. public-keys) of the originator
but also perform risk-assessment with regards to its truthfulness
and provenance. What matters in digital identities is not so much
the form of the identity (e.g. email-address; RSA public keys; X509

certificates[36,37]) but rather the *source of trust* for the provenance of the claimed identity.

The Bitcoin and PGP experience show that there is tension between the need for user privacy and for regulatory oversight/requirements with regards to the identification of the originator (sender) and recipient of value-transfer transactions. The latter is often referred to as "Know Your Customer" (KYC).

The notion of CoreID, personas and transaction-identities we propose in this chapter seeks to address this tension by approaching the challenge of identity through the appropriate combination of (a) highly private and accurate personal data as held by the Circle of Trust and the User (referred to as Core Identity); (b) the creation of a persona based on core assertions issued by the CoreID Provider as the representative of the Circle of Trust; and (c) the use of transaction-identities that may take the form of verifiable-anonymous identifiers. These components collectively establish a *chain of verifiability* (chain of provenance) that allows not only the relying party to validate the provenance of (anonymous) transaction-identities, but also provide entities in the ecosystem a way to satisfy regulatory requirements.

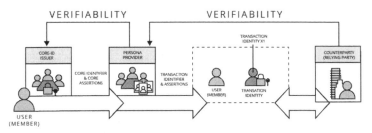

Figure 5: Chain of Verifiability and privacy preservation

The chain of verifiability or "chain of provenance" is a notion borrowed from the field of historical analysis and from that of art. In computer technology the term began to be commonly used in trusted computing[32] in the late 1990s to denote methods or mechanisms to prove the manufacturing origin of hardware and software components, specially components which perform crucial tasks in security-related computations (e.g. digital signatures, encryption). The notion of signed "manifests"[33] was used in this context as a means to capture the components that make-up a trusted platform.

The chain of verifiability can be implemented through a set of protocols and cryptographic mechanisms that allows a counterparty (relying-party) to assess the provenance of an anonymous-verifiable transaction identity while at the same time preserving the privacy of the user. Depending on the verification protocol, the counterparty may (i) engage the Persona Provider who issued the persona from which the transaction-identity was derived, or (ii) the counterparty may engage the (anonymous) user directly in a privacy-preserving manner (e.g. zero-knowledge proof exchanges).

The quality of assurance yielded from a verification instance of a given anonymous-verifiable transaction identity should be equivalent regardless as to whether the transaction identity was issued from the Persona Provider to the User, or whether the User self-derived (self-computed) the transaction identity from a set of cryptographic parameters bequeathed to the User by the Persona Provider. Additionally, the *form* of identity (e.g. public key pair, nonce, etc.) used for the given transaction medium (e.g. Internet, blockchain in a financial setting, etc.) should be user-selectable and should be independent from the means of proving the chain of provenance of the identity.

The freedom of users to use *anonymous but verifiable* transaction-identities should allow for different grades or strengths of anonymity to be deployed as function of the cryptographic constructs used to create the anonymous identities. This, in turn, allows Persona Providers – as the transaction-identity providers – to select the cryptographic algorithms that are appropriate to their business model, which may operate under differing regulatory requirements. Cryptographic algorithms and constructions, such as zero-knowledge proofs (ZKP) and group-membership protocols[29,30,31], provide promising building-blocks for a future identity ecosystem that preserves user privacy and satisfies regulatory requirements.

Related to anonymous-verifiable transaction identities, is the need for the counterparty to assess whether a claimed attribute assertion is truly bound to the transaction identity. We refer to this feature as *anonymous-verifiable attributes*. This capability allows a User to present to the counterparty an anonymous-verifiable transaction identity coupled with one or more anonymous attribute assertions.

The process of verifying an anonymous attribute assertion must also preserve the privacy of the User.

For blockchains and smart contracts which require the identities of transacting parties to be present in the executable smart contract, the use of anonymous-verifiable transaction identities and attributes provide a possible way forward in addressing the issue of privacy (of the transacting parties), which can be an acute problem in public/permission-less blockchains as well as private/permissioned blockchains.

SUMMARY: CALL TO ACTION

If the paradigm of blockchains is to positively revolutionize the world – in the way the IPv4 Internet has revolutionized the world – then a correspondingly new generation of digital identity technologies and infrastructures will need to be developed and deployed globally[8]. Such an identity scheme should understand the notion of core identities, personas and transaction identities. While core identities must never be used in transactions, the use of multiple personas and multiple transactions-identities should allow for different types transactions-identities to be derived depending on the type/medium of the transaction (e.g. Internet, blockchain, IoT, etc.).

There are a number of steps that can be initiated today towards engineering the building blocks of digital identity technologies for the future:

- **Open Algorithms for sharing personal data:** Develop open and safe algorithms/scripts for sharing personal data with the User's consent. Design principles founded on *Open Algorithms* (OPAL) can begin to be used by industry verticals in establishing Circles of Trust for sharing data for the purpose of creating core identities, personas and transaction-identities.

- **New legal trust frameworks for data sharing:** Since the sharing of data within a Circle of Trust is the foundation for core identities, new legal trust frameworks must be created specifically for data sharing. Such frameworks must address not only PII-rich personal data, but also corporate data (that pertain to the User) that may need to be shared within a Circle of Trust in a privacy-preserving manner.

Here, we believe that a number of industry verticals (e.g. Finance & Banking, Health, etc.) are suitably positioned to establish these new legal frameworks, which will in-turn benefit the Circle of Trust members through scaling of services and entrance into new mediums for transacting, such as blockchains and smart contracts.

- **Legal trust frameworks for providers of core identities, personas and transaction identities:** New legal frameworks for Identity Providers that create and manage core identities and personas for Users and organizations can begin to be designed and developed based on and extending existing trust frameworks[14,13]. Beyond addressing the syntax and limited semantics of digital identities as deployed today on the Internet, these new legal frameworks must capture and address the notion of personal data, core identities, chain of verifiability (provenance), and privacy of the user.

- **Standardization of anonymous-verifiable transaction identities and attributes:** A number of advanced cryptographic systems and constructions for anonymous-verifiable transaction identities can begin to be standardized, with specific instantiations developed for Internet transactions and for blockchain systems. Industry consortiums using specific types of blockchains or shared ledgers (e.g.[20]) can provide broader leadership in developing these privacy-preserving identities.

- **New incentive models for ecosystem participants:** With the emergence of IoT devices and the growth in data generated from consumer IoT devices (e.g. home appliances, medical devices, etc) the need for consumer privacy and therefore consent and "buy in" from consumers will become pressing matters. New models of incentives need to be developed which embraces the user/consumer as a stakeholder in the ecosystem and which incentivizes them to share higher quality data in a privacy-preserving manner.

CHAPTER 3
OPAL / ENIGMA

Yves-Alexandre de Montjoye, Thomas Hardjono,
Alex Pentland

We need new answers to questions around data privacy, data utility, and data trust. MIT Connection Science has proposed a multi-phase, open-source code project that we call OPAL /ENIGMA that we feel solves many of the problems that exist today.

One core issue derives from the fact that organizations (governments, companies, etc.) are holding vast amounts of customer data. They need to preserve data privacy while performing analytics and computations on data-sets, but advanced methods like homomorphic-encryption are impractical at large scale. The two-stage solution we propose is called OPAL/ENIGMA[1].

The first stage is OPAL, which stands for Open Algorithms, which was originally developed by de Montjoye and Pentland at MIT[2] and by Descordes at Orange, and now has widespread support and involvement (see http:/opalproject.org). This system minimizes and controls data sharing by two simple techniques. The first technique is that algorithms are sent to the data stores to be evaluated behind existing firewalls instead of sending data to be processed elsewhere. Only publically approved algorithms are allowed. The consequence is that only answers that are deemed safe are shared out of existing databases, not the data itself. The second technique is to log the identities, algorithms, and results on a secure distributed ledger such as a blockchain. This provides incorruptible transparency and accountability.

The ENIGMA system takes the idea of OPAL and adds encryption; it was originally developed at MIT by Zyskind, Nathan and Pentland[3] (see ENIGMA.media.mit.edu). In the ENIGMA system data is encrypted at all times, and computation is done on encrypted data without decrypting it. To accomplish this we split data-sets into encrypted shares and disperse shares to the distributed-nodes of a distributed ledger (e.g., a blockchain). By using special algorithms to perform computation on shares, and employing secure Multi-Party Computation (sMPC), we can leave data encrypted while making it useful, and the distributed nodes are resilient against attacks.

OPAL and ENIGMA allow for greater trust in what computations are performed, because algorithms are transparently and publically evaluated before they are approved and implemented. We are currently building on a five-year technical roadmap, from early instantiations of OPAL (Open Algorithms) through full secure multiparty computation with secret sharing (ENIGMA).

This chapter will explore these powerful new systems.

Data, the most valuable commodity in the 21st century

The term "datafication" was coined to describe the consequences of the digital revolution: the growing generation, collection and storage of digital information concerning all aspects of the physical world (including earth activity, weather, climate, and biosphere), human lives and activities (including DNA, vital signs, consumption, and credit scores), and societal patterns (including communications, economic activity, and mobility). The datafication of the world is fueled by the automatic generation of data through the billions of digital devices that surround us: cellphones and tablets, e-devices, security cameras, credit cards, badges and satellites. However, little of the generated information is actually used to improve people's lives or in the design of better public policies.

The flow of information resulting from this datafication process is mainly stored within data centers, as a commodity, typically legally owned by the private companies collecting them – telecom operators, social media companies, or banks, among others.   These data are analyzed for internal and commercial purposes – think of how Amazon or Facebook operates, for example – and hold tremendous value. Companies whose investments, innovations and systems contribute to generating and storing these data cannot simply surrender it.

But many private companies do not realize the public good value of these data – including how they could benefit from opening up "some" of their data if it helps to grow economies or prevent epidemics[7,8]. Even when they do, they face not only commercial but also ethical and legal incentives not to open up their data. Indeed, not all data should be open. Personal data collected through our usage of social networks, our mobile phone activities, sensors and connected devices all inform pretty accurately our way of life: our location, whether real time or historical; the people we communicate with; the content of our private messages or emails; our heart rate, or even our most intimate feelings – we wouldn't like such information to be publicly available.

Meanwhile, the case for opening and using data has become clearer in recent years. First, the "open data movement" has shown how opening up data can foster public innovation, foster civic engagement, accountability and transparency. Second, a handful of companies – chief of which telecom operators, including Orange, Telefónica and

Telecom Italia – have experimented with "data challenges," whereby some data are made available to researchers as part of a controlled experiment.

The successes and results of these challenges revealed and stirred up growing demands for more "private" data to be made available. Some, such as Kenneth Cukier, the Economist's senior editor for data and digital, even consider that not using these data is "the moral equivalent of burning books." But the dilemma remained between privacy and utility; between commercial, individual and societal considerations, and so on.

Which data should be accessed, for what and by whom?

Two recent developments further complicate the debate. One is the finding that "anonymizing" data was much harder than previously thought – the uniqueness of our behaviors and the interconnectedness of datasets in which we appear, makes "re-identifiability" possible[9]. This all but rules out the option of "simply" releasing personal data without personally identifiable information as a long-term solution.

Another development was the "Facebook emotion study," where the social media giant used data and manipulated the newsfeeds of hundreds of thousands of users as part of an experiment that was perfectly legal but deemed unethical – putting the notion of what "informed consent" meant and entailed back at the forefront of these debates.

The concern that algorithms operate as "black boxes" that could embed and help entrench biases and discriminations has also gained ground. And the pressures to use these data to improve people's lives will most likely continue growing – including in support of the Sustainable Development Goals – alongside people's demand to <u>have greater control over this use</u> – in ways that respect individual and <u>group privacies</u>, commercial interests, and of course prevailing legal standards.

What is the need for OPAL and ENIGMA?

Technological and institutional innovations have opened up a new world of data production, dissemination, and analysis. The volume of data in the world is increasing rapidly both from traditional and new sources, as experimentation, innovation, and adaptation make possible new, more immediate, and often more detailed ways of collecting and accessing it – for example through mobile phones. Increased demand for data has spread to a greater range of stakeholders (including governments, private companies, academics, civil society, etc.), along with rising expectations for how data can and should be used to enhance decision-making and transform lives particularly when used for development and policy-making.

Historically, the data and development ecosystem has been made up of two types of actors: data providers and consumers. This paradigm is however shifting with the appearance of stakeholders that serve both roles in the private and public sectors and trust between them need to be strengthened. Official frameworks and principles around the ethics of sharing and use of many new sources of data have not yet been established. The potential of creating secure and scalable infrastructure and mechanisms not only facilitates collaboration among actors in the global data ecosystem but also allows more ethical and equitable practices and standards.

The OPAL and ENIGMA projects are born from the observation that even as the social value of data collected by private companies has been demonstrated by numerous academic studies, access to this day remains legitimately constrained by ethical, political, legal and commercial considerations. Various initiatives such as Orange D4D challenges or 'Hackathons' organized especially by Telefónica or Telecom Italia operators have enabled researchers to work on heavily limited mobile phone data; in other cases, academic initiatives have had access to more granular data through specific agreements that rely heavily on personal relationships. These terms do not allow for the scalability, systemization and commitment of a wide range of stakeholders necessary for the responsible use of data or for harnessing the full potential of social value from such data.

To crack the privacy problem, we are looking to change the paradigm.

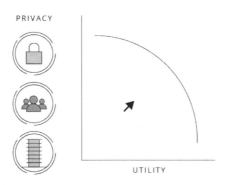

OPAL: THE FIRST STAGE OF USING DATA FOR GOOD

To address the complex challenge of data access, Orange, MIT Connection Science, Data-Pop Alliance, Imperial College London, and the World Economic Forum – supported by Agence Française de Développement (AFD) and the World Bank – are developing a platform to unleash the power of "big data" held by private companies for public good in a privacy preserving, commercially sensible, stable, scalable and sustainable manner.

In its initial phase of deployment, the Open Algorithms project (OPAL) will focus on a small set of countries in Latin America, Africa and Asia, with technical support from a wide range of partners including PARIS21, Microsoft, and Deloitte Consulting LLP.

OPAL's core will consist of an open technology platform and open algorithms running directly on the servers of partner companies, behind their firewalls, to extract key development indicators of relevance for a wide range of potential users, including national statistical offices, ministries, civil society organizations, media organizations, etc. Examples of potential indicators and maps produced with greater frequency and levels of geographic granularity currently available include poverty, literacy, population density, social cohesion – all on which the literature has shown that "big data" analysis could shed light.

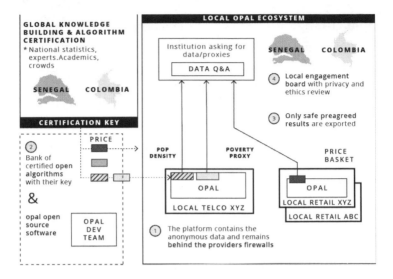

Figure: The OPAL platform and ecosystem

The OPAL platform will start with mobile telecommunications data with operations in four countries by mid- 2017 and expected deployment globally by 2020. This project is a collaboration between a wide range of actors of the data and development ecosystem— joining forces to address a longstanding challenge that impedes the positive impact that data could have on social progress. Ultimately, the project aims to catalyze public-private data sharing to support evidence-based policy making and near-term decision-making. This work would collaboratively support the larger aims of the "Data Revolution" to achieve the Sustainable Development Goals.

OPAL's core will consist of an open platform and set of algorithms that can be run on the servers of partner companies, behind their firewalls, to extract key development indicators and operational data of relevance for a wide range of potential users.

While OPAL is a generic solution, the current proposal proposes to develop and apply it to the mobile telecommunications sector.

As a "platform" to unleash the power of these "big data" held by private companies for public good, the Agence Française de Développement (AFD) and the World Bank is supporting OPAL with three key aims:

1.   To engage with data providers, users and analysts at all stages of its development, including during the development of algorithms.

2.   Contribute to building local capacities, connections and help shape the future technological, political, ethical and legal frameworks that will govern the local collection, control and use of "big data" to foster social progress.
      By "sending the code to the data" rather than the other way around, OPAL seeks to address these challenges and spur dialogues and develop data services on the basis of greater trust between all parties involved – including between citizens, official statistical systems and private corporations.

3.   To build data literacy among users and partners; not just data literacy defined as "the ability to use data," but conceptualized in a broader and deeper sense as literacy in the age of data and defined as "the ability to constructively engage in society through and about data." In the 21st century, being "data literate" in that sense will be as much a fundamental human capability as a useful professional skill set; both an enabler and

marker of human agency.

Mass data literacy will be as essential to development and democracy as mass literacy has been during the 20th century. Building this kind of data literacy across institutions and groups will require large-scale sustained initiatives and investments that have not yet materialized.

Initially these capacities would be tailored to address the needs of National Statistical Offices to gain access to non-traditional data sources. This community of stakeholders consists of influential, data-literate and supportive actors that can lay the foundations for expanding the project to other use cases and can be used to scale up solutions. They are in contact with Ministries and can promote data to drive change in developing countries which, are in critical need of new data and metrics, more efficient ways to measure and track indicators, and capacity building support.

Value creation happens for many parties in OPAL platforms. The general mechanism will be model including data providers, algorithm providers and a network of sustainable Data Services. There will inevitably be many commercial use cases of OPAL data (e.g. where to position a new bank agency, where tourists are located this week, how to target the high population densities with a media campaign, etc.). We consider this an opportunity to increase the viability of the Data Ecosystem.

Who is involved in the OPAL deployment?

The project is currently led by a small number of key individuals representing key organizations—referred to as the 'Executive Committee'–and managed by the Overseas Development Institute (ODI):

1.   Nicolas de Cordes for Orange, working with Zbigniew
      Smoreda, Stefania Rubrichi, Cezari Ziemlicki
2.   Dr. Yves-Alexandre de Montjoye for Imperial College London
      and MIT, working with Brian Sweatt
3.   William Hoffman, for the World Economic Forum USA
      Emmanuel Letouzé for Data-Pop Alliance, working with Natalie
      Shoup
4.   Prof. Alex Pentland for MIT

with input and guidance from: Claire Melamed, Overseas
Development Institute; Johannes Jütting, PARIS21; Jessica Espey, SDSN;
Sabrina Juran, UNFPA; Marc Levy, CIESIN; Rick Lievin Microsoft; Pierre
Gauthier TMForum.

ENIGMA: A DECENTRALIZED, ENCRYPTED DATA ECOLOGY

How are we to we evolve a trusted data sharing mechanism that is
intrinsically secure and which supports data ownership and privacy
as first-class priorities?   By minimizing data exposure and providing
public transparency and accountability the OPAL project provides the
first step. However we know that whenever data is unencrypted, it
can be (and increasingly is) attacked and stolen. For this reasons we
are creating ENIGMA[3], a decentralized computation platform enabling
different parties to jointly store and run computations on data while
keeping the data completely private. Such technology allows us to
realize data sharing opportunities, while respecting security concerns
by use of distributed ledger (blockchain) protocols.

From the user's perspective, ENIGMA is a cloud that ensures both
privacy and integrity of their data. The system also allows any type
of computation to be outsourced to the cloud while guaranteeing the

privacy of the underlying data and the correctness of the result. A core feature in the system is that it allows the data owners to define and control who can query it, thus ensuring that the approved parties only learn the output. Moreover, no other data leaks in the process to any other party.

The ENIGMA cloud itself is comprised of a network of computers that store and execute queries. Using secure multi-party computation[10,11,12] (MPC), each computer only sees random pieces of the data, a fact that prevents information leaks. Furthermore, queries carry a micro-payment for the computing resources as well as to those users whose data is queried, thus providing the foundation for the rise of a data market.

To illustrate how the platform works, consider the following example: a group of data analysts of an insurance company wishes to test a model that leverages people's mobile phone data. Instead of sharing their raw data with the data analysts in the insurance company, the users can securely store their data in ENIGMA, and only provide the data analysts with a permission to execute their study. The data analysts are thus able to execute their code and obtain the results, but nothing else. In the process, the users are compensated for having given access to their data and the computers in the network are paid for their computing resources.

ENIGMA Design Overview

Three types of entities are defined in ENIGMA, and each can play multiple roles (see Figure 1). Owners are those sharing their data into the system and controlling who can query it; services, if approved, can query the data without learning anything else beyond the answer to their query; and parties (or computing parties) are the nodes that provide computational and storage resources, but only ever see encrypted or random bits of information. In addition, all entities are connected to a blockchain as described below.

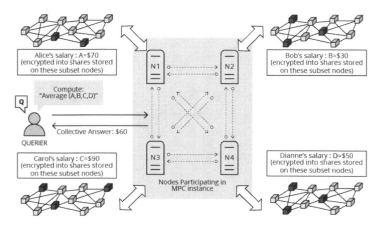

Overview of ENIGMA's decentralized platform.

When owners share data, the data is split into several random pieces called *shares*. Shares are created in a process of secret-sharing and perfectly hide the underlying data while maintaining some necessary properties allowing them to later be queried in this masked form. Since users in ENIGMA are owners of their data, we need a trusted database to publicly store a proof of who owns which data. However, trusting a centralized database to attest your ownership is arguably no better than trusting a server to hold your data. Instead, we use the blockchain as a decentralized secure database that is not owned by any party.

Our solution is based on Zyskind et al.[3], which also allows an owner to designate which services can access its data and under what conditions. This way, when a service requests a computation, parties can query the blockchain and ensure that it holds the appropriate permissions. Note that parties are only paid when they provide computing resources to an authorized service, so they have no incentive to provide work for unauthorized entities, e.g., such behavior is penalized.

In addition to being a secure and distributed public database, the blockchain is also used to facilitate payments from services to computing parties and owners, while enforcing correct permissions and verifying that queries execute correctly. The latter allows for more efficient MPC protocols, since validating that a distributed computation terminated successfully is often the most expensive part of the protocol. In our system, such parts are delegated to the blockchain and can be post-processed after the computation finishes and the result is made available to the service. Below we describe in more detail the innards of blockchain technology and explain how it enables transferring value, as well as storing information in a distributed and immutable manner that ensures data-integrity.

Distributed Ledger Technology

A distributed ledger such as a blockchain is a chronological public database of transactions recorded by a network of computers and is organized into smaller datasets referred to as "blocks". Each block contains information about a certain number of transactions, a reference to the preceding block in the blockchain, as well as an answer to a computationally-hard mathematical puzzle used to prove that the consensus node - a term used to refer to computers constructing blocks in the network - has put sufficient work (or other qualifying property) into building that block. A copy of the blockchain is stored on every computer in the network and new blocks are broadcasted and propagated through the network, where every computer independently validates each incoming block and its encompassed transactions before appending it to its local copy of the blockchain. This procedure ensures all computers (eventually) store the same database. Validating transactions boils down to ensuring that they are legitimate and do not attempt to spend funds that do not exist or double-spend funds that have been used in previous transactions.

This procedure also implicitly ensures that only legitimate transactions are recorded into a blockchain, and that there is a network-wide consensus on which transactions are valid. Consensus within the network is achieved through different voting mechanisms, the most common of which is Proof of Work, which depends on the amount of processing power donated to the network. After a block has been added to the blockchain, it can no longer be deleted and the transactions it contains can be accessed and verified by everyone on the network. It becomes a permanent record that all of the computers on the network can use to coordinate an action or verify an event.

A blockchain forces information traveling over a network of computers to become more transparent and verifiable using mathematical problems that require significant computational power to solve. This makes it harder for potential attackers to corrupt a shared database with false information, unless the attacker owns a majority of the computational power of the entire network. Blockchain protocols thus ensure that transactions on a blockchain are valid and never recorded to the shared repository more than once, enabling people to coordinate individual transactions in a decentralized manner without the need to rely on a trusted authority to verify and clear all transactions. Note that nowadays, a blockchain can be used to store arbitrary data (with severe limitations on size) in transactions and the conditions in which a transaction is deemed valid can be programmed (sometime referred to as a 'smart contract'). This ability is key in allowing ENIGMA to enforce stronger conditions, such as recording owners and permissions, and only validating payments sent from approved services requesting computations that terminate successfully.

From OPAL to ENGIMA

The goal of both OPAL and ENIGMA is to provide privacy-preserving sharing of data across multiple data repositories, belonging to individuals and organizations alike. These two approaches represent two ends of a spectrum, and where each phase within the spectrum suitability within different application areas. The following figure summarizes the three phases.

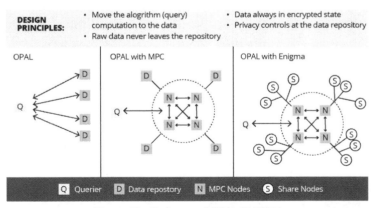

Figure: The 3 phases of OPAL/ENIGMA

(a) Phase I: OPAL

OPAL introduces the new paradigm of moving the queries ("algorithms") to the data repositories, where each data repository participating in the query-computation performs all computations themselves behind their firewalls. Raw data is never exported, and each repository has the opportunity to filter responses and return only safe-answers.

Additionally, each repository has the opportunity to introduce artificial intelligence and machine learning as an additional mechanism to protect privacy. Such systems and tools allow a repository to detect if multiple queries from the same querier results in the compromise of PII information.

The task of collating the responses from each repository is the responsibility of the querier, and each data repository may not be aware that the querier is engaging multiple data repositories. Thus, the notion of collective-computation is absent in the pure OPAL scheme.

(b) Phase II: OPAL with MPC

Multi Party Computation (MPC) introduces the ability of repositories to collectively perform a query computation that yields some statistical results, but without revealing raw data. Each repository maintains its own plaintext data in a centralized fashion (as in the pure OPAL case), and may use data loss prevention (DLP) mechanisms to prevent attacks.

To move from the pure OPAL design to using OPAL with MPC, a data repository must augment its system with a group compatible MPC cryptographic scheme to achieve interoperability. Depending on the precise scheme, participating in a given MPC instance may result in increased computation power consumption and increase in messaging traffic among the participants of the MPC instance.

A benefit of using MPC is the ability of each member of the MPC instance to know which member (i.e. data repository) was involved in the computation, and to obtain some assurance that all members in the computation instance are seeing the same final result of the computation. This is something that the pure OPAL design is not able to achieve with the querier-centric design.

(c) Phase III: OPAL with ENIGMA

ENIGMA itself incorporates the notion of Multi Party Computation (as in OPAL with MPC), but extends it further by encrypting each data item in a repository using a linear secrets sharing scheme[3] (LSSS) in such a way that collectively computation in an MPC instance can be performed on these encrypted shares (without decrypting them). For example, a linear secret sharing scheme may encrypt a data item into M shares (e.g. 11 shares) where a threshold of any N (e.g. any 7 of 11 shares) is needed to reconstruct the original data item.

Encrypting data items into multiple shares has the immediate benefit that the centralized data store approach is no longer needed and shares can be dispersed to physically distributed locations. This physical distribution reduces the surface of attack because now the attacker needs to compromise at least N (e.g. 7) locations, something which is considerably harder than compromising one centralized data repository.

The cost of moving from the OPAL to OPAL with ENIGMA consists in the addition of new infrastructures, not only to manage the MPC computations and messaging, but also to manage the shares relating to each data item. Thus, the OPAL/ENIGMA approach provides increased security at the cost of increased complexity in infrastructure technology.

CHAPTER 4

Reshaping the Social Contract:
The New Deal on Data

Daniel "Dazza" Greenwood,
Arkadiusz Stopczynski, Brian Sweatt,
Thomas Hardjono and Alex Pentland

In order to realize the promise of a Data for Good society and to reduce the potential risk to individuals, institutions are updating the operational frameworks which govern the business, legal, and technical dimensions of their internal organizations. In this chapter we outline ways to support the emergence of such a society within the framework of the New Deal on Data, and describe future directions for research and development. In our view, the traditional control points relied on as part of corporate governance, management oversight, legal compliance, and enterprise architecture must evolve and expand to match operational frameworks for big data. These controls must support and reflect greater user control over personal data, as well as large-scale interoperability for data sharing between and among institutions. The core capabilities of these controls should include responsive rule-based systems governance and fine-grained authorizations for distributed rights management.

The New Deal on Data

The digital breadcrumbs we leave behind are clues to who we are, what we do, and what we want. This makes personal data – data about individuals – immensely valuable, both for public good and for private companies. The ability to see the details of so many interactions is also immensely powerful and can be used for good or for ill. Therefore, protecting personal privacy and freedom is critical to our future success as a society. We need to enable more data sharing for the public good; at the same time, we need to do a much better job of protecting the privacy of individuals.

A successful data-driven society must be able to guarantee that our data will not be abused – perhaps especially that government will not abuse the power conferred by access to such fine-grained data.

There are many ways in which abuses might be directly targeted –
from imposing higher insurance rates based on individual shopping
history,[11] to creating problems for the entire society, by limiting user
choices and enclosing users in information bubbles.[12] To achieve the
potential for a new society, we require the New Deal on Data, which
describes workable guarantees that the data needed for public good is
readily available while at the same time protecting the citizenry.[13]

The key insight behind the New Deal on Data is that our data is
worth more when shared. Aggregate data – averaged, combined
across population, and often distilled to high-level features – can
be used to inform improvements in systems such as public health,
transportation, and government. For instance, we have demonstrated
that data about the way we behave and where we go can be used to
minimize the spread of infectious disease.[14] Our research has also
shown how digital breadcrumbs can be used to track the spread of
influenza from person to person on an individual level. And the public
good can be served as a result: if we can see it, we can also stop it.
Similarly, if we are worried about global warming, shared, aggregated
data can reveal how patterns of mobility relate to productivity.[15] This,
in turn, equips us to design cities that are more productive and, at the
same time, more energy efficient. However, to obtain these results
and make a greener world, we must be able to see people moving
around; this depends on having many people willing to contribute
their data, if only anonymously and in aggregate. In addition, the
Big Data transformation can help society find efficient means of
governance by providing tools to analyze and understand what needs
to be done, and to reach consensus on how to do it. This goes beyond
simply creating more communication platforms; the assumption that
more interaction between users will produce better decisions may be

very misleading. Although in recent years, we have seen impressive uses of social networks for better organization in society, for example during political protests.[16] We are far from even starting to reach consensus about the big problems: epidemics, climate change, pollution – big data can help us achieve such goals.

However, to enable the sharing of personal data and experiences, we need secure technology and regulation that allows individuals to safely and conveniently share personal information with each other, with corporations, and with government. Consequently, the heart of the New Deal on Data must be to provide both regulatory standards and financial incentives enticing owners to share data, while at the same time serving the interests of individuals and society at large. We must promote greater idea flow among individuals, not just within corporations or government departments.

Unfortunately, today most personal data are siloed in private companies and therefore largely unavailable. Private organizations collect the vast majority of personal data in the form of mobility patterns, financial transactions, and phone and Internet communications. These data must not remain the exclusive domain of private companies, because they are then less likely to contribute to the common good; private organizations must be key players in the New Deal on Data. Likewise, this data should not become the exclusive domain of the government. The entities who should be empowered to share and make decisions about their data are the people themselves: users, participants, citizens. We can involve both experts and use the wisdom of crowds – users themselves interested in improving society.

Personal Data: Emergence of a New Asset Class

One of the first steps to promoting liquidity in land and commodity markets is to guarantee ownership rights so that people can safely buy and sell. Similarly, a first step toward creating more ideas and greater flow of ideas – idea liquidity – is to define ownership rights. The only politically viable course is to give individual citizens key rights over data that are about them, the type of rights that have undergirded the European Union's Privacy Directive since 1995.[17] We need to recognize personal data as a valuable asset of the individual, which can be given to companies and government in return for services.

We can draw the definition of ownership from English common law on ownership rights of possession, use, and disposal:

- You have the right to possess data about yourself. Regardless of what entity collects the data, the data belong to you, and you can access your data at any time. Data collectors thus play a role akin to a bank, managing data on behalf of their 'customers'.
- You have the right to full control over the use of your data. The terms of use must be opt in and clearly explained in plain language. If you are not happy with the way a company uses your data, you can remove the data, just as you would close your account with a bank that is not providing satisfactory service.
- You have the right to dispose of or distribute your data. You have the option to have data about you destroyed or redeployed elsewhere.

Individual rights to personal data must be balanced with the need of corporations and governments to use certain data- account activity, billing information, and the like to run their day-to-day operations.

The New Deal on Data therefore gives individuals the right to possess, control, and dispose of copies of these required operational data, along with copies of the incidental data collected about the individual, such as location and similar context. These ownership rights are not exactly the same as literal ownership under modern law; the practical effect is that disputes are resolved in a different, simpler manner than would be the case for land ownership disputes, for example.

In 2007, one author (AP) first proposed the New Deal on Data to the World Economic Forum.[18] Since then, this idea has run through various discussions and eventually helped to shape the 2012 Consumer Data Bill of Rights in the United States, along with a matching declaration on Personal Data Rights in the European Union.

The World Economic Forum (WEF) echoed the European Consumer Commissioner, Meglena Kuneva, in dubbing personal data the 'new oil' or new resource of the 21st century.[19] The 'personal data sector' of the economy today is in its infancy, its state akin to the oil industry during the late 1890s. Productive collaboration between government (building the state-owned freeways), the private sector (mining and refining oil, building automobiles), and the citizens (the user-base of these services) allowed developed nations to expand their economies by creating new markets adjacent to the automobile and oil industries.

If personal data, as the new oil, is to reach its global economic potential, productive collaboration is needed between all stakeholders in the establishment of a personal data ecosystem. A number of fundamental uncertainties exist, however, about privacy, property, global governance, human rights – essentially about who should benefit from the products and services built on personal data.[20] The rapid rate of technological change and commercialization in the use of personal data is undermining end-user confidence and trust.

The current personal data ecosystem is feudal, fragmented, and inefficient. Too much leverage is currently accorded to service providers that enroll and register end -users. Their siloed repositories of personal data exemplify the fragmentation of the ecosystem, containing data of varying qualities; some are attributes of persons that are unverified, while others represent higher quality data that have been cross-correlated with other data points of the end-user. For many individuals, the risks and liabilities of the current ecosystem exceed the economic returns. Besides not having the infrastructure and tools to manage personal data, many end-users simply do not see the benefit of fully participating. Personal privacy concerns are thus addressed inadequately at best, or simply overlooked in the majority of cases. Current technologies and laws fall short of providing the legal and technical infrastructure needed to support a well-functioning digital economy.

Recently, we have seen the challenges, but also the feasibility of opening private big data. In the Data for Development (D4D) Challenge (http:// www.d4d.orange.com), the telecommunication operator, Orange, opened access to a large dataset of call detail records from the Ivory Coast. Working with the data as part of a challenge, teams of researchers came up with life-changing insights for the country. For example, one team developed a model for how disease spreads in the country and demonstrated that information campaigns based on one-to-one phone conversations among members of social groups can be an effective countermeasure.[21] Data release must be carefully done, however; as we have seen in several cases, such as the Netflix

Prize privacy disaster[22] and other similar privacy breaches,[23] true anonymization is extremely hard – recent research by de Montjoye et al. and others [24-25] has shown that even though human beings are highly predictable, we are also unique. Having access to one dataset may be enough to uniquely fingerprint someone based on just a few data points, and this fingerprint can be used to discover their true identity. In releasing and analyzing the D4D data, the privacy of the people who generated the data was protected not only by technical means, such as removal of personally identifiable information (PII), but also by legal means, with the researchers signing an agreement that they would not use the data for re-identification or other nefarious purposes. Opening data from the silos by publishing static datasets – collected at some point and unchanging – is important, but it is only the first step. We can do even more when data is available in real time and can become part of a society`s nervous system. Epidemics can be monitored and prevented in real time,[26] underperforming students can be helped, and people with health risks can be treated before they get sick.[27]

The report of the World Economic Forum[28] suggests a way forward by identifying useful areas on which to focus efforts:

- *Alignment of key stakeholders:* Citizens, the private sector, and the public sector need to work in support of one another. Efforts such as NSTIC[29] in the United States – albeit still in its infancy – represent a promising direction for global collaboration.
- *Viewing 'data as money':* There needs to be a new mindset, in which an individual's personal data items are viewed and treated in the same way as their money. These personal data items would reside in an 'account' (like a bank account) where they would be controlled, managed, exchanged, and accounted for just as

personal banking services operate today.

- *End-user centricity* : All entities in the ecosystem need to recognize end-users as vital and independent stakeholders in the co-creation and exchange of services and experiences. Efforts such as the User Managed Access (UMA) initiative[30] provide examples of system design that are user-centric and managed by the user.

Enforcing the New Deal on Data

How can we enforce this New Deal? The threat of legal action is important, but not sufficient; if you cannot see abuses, you cannot prosecute them. Enforcement can be addressed significantly without prosecution or public statute or regulation. In many fields, companies and governments rely on rules governing common business, legal, and technical (BLT) practices to create effective self-organization and enforcement. This approach holds promise as a method by which institutional controls can form a reliable operational framework for big data, privacy, and access.

One current best practice is a system of data sharing called a 'trust network', a combination of networked computers and legal rules defining and governing expectations regarding data. For personal data, these networks of technical and legal rules keep track of user permissions for each piece of data and act as a legal contract, specifying what happens in case of a violation. For example, in a trust network all personal data can have attached labels specifying where the data come from and what they can and cannot be used for. These labels are exactly matched by the terms in the legal contracts between all of the participants, stating penalties for not obeying them. The rules can – and often do – reference or require audits of relevant systems and data use, demonstrating how traditional internal controls can be leveraged as part of the transition to more novel trust models. A well-designed trust network, elegantly integrated computer and legal rules, allows automatic auditing of data use and allows individuals to change their permissions and withdraw data.

The mechanism for establishing and operating a trust network is to create system rules for the applications, service providers, data, and the users themselves. System rules are sometimes called 'operating regulations' in the credit card context, 'trust frameworks' in the identity federation context, or 'trading partner agreements' in a supply value chain context. Several multiparty shared architectural and contractual rules create binding obligations and enforceable expectations on all participants in scalable networks. Furthermore, the design of the system rules allows participants to be widely distributed across heterogeneous business ownership boundaries, legal governance structures, and technical security domains. However, the parties need not conform in all or even most aspects of their basic roles, relationships, and activities in order to connect to a trust network. Cross-domain trusted systems must – by their nature – focus enforceable rules narrowly on commonly agreed items in order for that network to achieve its purpose.

For example, institutions participating in credit card and automated clearing house networks are subject to profoundly different sets of regulations, business practices, economic conditions, and social expectations. The network rules focus on the topmost agreed items affecting interoperability, reciprocity, risk, and revenue allocation. The knowledge that fundamental rules are subject to enforcement action is one of the foundations of trust and a motivation to prevent or address violations before they trigger penalties. A clear example of this approach can be found in the Visa Operating Rules, which cover a vast global real-time network of parties agreeing to rules governing their roles in the system as merchants, banks, transaction processors, individual or business card holders, and other key system roles.

Such rules have made the interbank money transfer system among the safest systems in the world and the backbone for daily exchanges of trillions of dollars, but until recently those were only for the 'big guys'.[31] To give individuals a similarly safe method of managing personal data, the Human Dynamics group at MIT, in partnership with the Institute for Data Driven Design (co-founded by John Clippinger and one author (AP)) have helped to build an open Personal Data Store (openPDS).[32] The openPDS is a consumer version of a personal cloud trust network now being tested with a variety of industry and government partners. The aim is to make sharing personal data as safe and secure as transferring money between banks.

When dealing with data intended to be accessible over networks – whether big, personal, or otherwise – the traditional container of an institution makes less and less sense. Institutional controls apply, by definition, to some type of institutional entity such as a business, governmental, or religious organization. A synopsis of all the BLT facts and circumstances surrounding big data is necessary in order to know what access, confidentiality, and other expectations exist; the relevant contextual aspects of big data at one institution are often profoundly different from those at another. As more and more organizations use and rely on big data, a single formula for institutional controls will not work for increasingly heterogeneous BLT environments.

The capacity to apply appropriate methods of enforcement for a trust network depends on clear understanding and agreement among the parties about the purpose of the system and the respective roles or expectations of those connecting as participants. Therefore, some contextual anchor is needed to have a clear basis for establishing an operational framework and institutional controls appropriate for big data.

Transitioning End-User Assent Practices

The way users grant authorization to share their data is not a trivial matter. The flow of personal information such as location data, purchases, and health records can be very complex. Every tweet, geotagged picture, phone call, or purchase with credit card provides the user's location not only to the primary service, but also to all the applications and services that have been authorized to access and reuse these data. The authorization may come from the end-user or be granted by the collecting service, based on umbrella terms of service that cover reuse of the data. Implementation of such flows was a crucial part of the Web 2.0 revolution, realized with RESTful APIs, mash-ups, and authorization-based access. The way personal data travels between services has arguably become too complex for a user to handle and manage.

Increasing the range of data controlled by the user and the granularity of this control is meaningless if it cannot be exercised in an informed way. For many years, a poor model has been provided by End User License Agreements (EULAs), long incomprehensible texts that are accepted blindly by users trusting they have not agreed to anything that could harm them. The process of granting meaningful authorization cannot be too complex, as it would prevent a user from understanding her decisions. At the same time, it cannot be too simplistic, as it may not sufficiently convey the weight of the privacy-related decisions it captures. It is a challenge in itself to build end-user assent systems that allow users to understand and adjust their privacy settings.

This gap between the interface – single click – and the effect can render data ownership meaningless; one click may wrench people and their data into systems and rules that are antithetical to fair information practices, as is prevalent with today's end-user licenses in cloud services or applications. Managing the long-term tensions fueled by 'old deal' systems operating simultaneously with the New Deal is an important design and migration challenge during the transition to a Big Data economy. During this transition and after the New Deal on Data is no longer new, personal data must continue to flow in order to be useful. Protecting the data of people outside of directly user-controlled domains is very hard without a combination of cost-effective and useful business practices, legal rules, and technical solutions.

We envision 'living informed consent', where the user is entitled to know what data is being collected about her by which entities, empowered to understand the implications of data sharing, and finally put in charge of the sharing authorizations. We suggest that readers ask themselves a question: Which services know which city I am in today? Google? Apple? Twitter? Amazon? Facebook? Flickr? Some app I authorized a few years ago to access my Facebook check-ins and have since forgotten about? This is an example of a fundamental question related to user privacy and assent, and yet finding an accurate answer can be surprisingly difficult in today's ecosystem. We can hope that most services treat data responsibly and according to user authorizations. In the complex network of data flows, however, it is relatively easy for data to leak to careless or malicious services.[33] We need to build solutions that help users to make well-informed decisions about data sharing in this environment.

Big Data and Personal Data Institutional Controls

The concept of 'institutional controls' refers to safeguards and protections implemented through legal, policy, governance, and other measures that are not solely technical, engineering, or mechanical. Institutional controls in the context of big data can perhaps best be understood by examining how such controls have been applied to other domains, most prevalently in the field of environmental regulation. A good example of how this concept supports and reflects the goals and objectives of environmental regulation can be found in the policy documents of the Environmental Protection Agency (EPA), which gives the following definition in its Institutional Controls Glossary:

Institutional Controls – Non-engineering measures intended to affect human activities in such a way as to prevent or reduce exposure to hazardous substances. They are almost always used in conjunction with, or as a supplement to, other measures such as waste treatment or containment. There are four categories of institutional controls: governmental controls; proprietary controls; enforcement tools; and informational devices.[34]

The concept of an 'institutional control boundary' is especially clarifying and powerful when applied to the networked and digital boundaries of an institution. In the context of Florida's environmental regulation, the phrase is applied when a property owner's risk management and clean-up responsibilities extend beyond the area defined by the physical property boundary. For example, a recent University of Florida report on clean-up target levels (CTLs) states, "in some rare situations, the institutional control boundary at which default CTLs must be met can extend beyond the site property boundary."[35]

When institutional controls apply to "separately owned neighboring properties" a number of possibilities arise that are very relevant to management of personal data across legal, business, and other systemic boundaries. Requiring the party responsible for site clean-up to use "best efforts" to attain agreement from the neighboring owners to institute the relevant institutional controls is perhaps the most direct and least prescriptive approach. When direct negotiated agreement is unsuccessful, then use of third-party neutrals to resolve disagreements regarding institutional controls can be required. If necessary, environmental regulation can force the acquisition of neighboring land by compelling the party responsible to purchase the other property or by purchase of the property directly by the EPA.[36]

In the context of big data, institutional controls are seldom, if ever, imposed through government regulatory frameworks such as are seen in environmental waste management oversight by the EPA.[37] Rather, institutions applying measures constituting institutional controls in the big data and related information technology and enterprise architecture contexts will typically employ governance safeguards, business practices, legal contracts, technical security, reporting, and audit programs and various risk management measures.

Inevitably, institutional controls for big data will have to operate effectively across institutional boundaries, just as environmental waste management must sometimes be applied across real property boundaries and may subject multiple different owners to enforcement actions corresponding to the applicable controls. Short of government regulation, the use of system rules as a general model is one widely understood, accepted, and efficient method for defining, agreeing, and enforcing institutional and other controls across BLT domains of ownership, governance, and operation.

Following on from the World Economic Forum's recommendation to treat personal data stores in the manner of bank accounts,[38] a number of infrastructure improvements need to be realized if the personal data ecosystem is to flourish and deliver new economic opportunities:

- **New global data provenance network:** In order for personal data stores to be treated like bank accounts, origin information regarding data items coming into the data store must be maintained.[39] In other words, the provenance of all data items must be accounted for by the IT infrastructure on which the personal data store operates. The databases must then be interconnected in order to provide a resilient, scalable platform for audit and accounting systems to track and reconcile the movement of personal data from different data stores.

- **Trust network for computational law:** For trust to be established between parties who wish to exchange personal data, some degree of 'computational law' technology may have to be integrated into the design of personal data systems. This technology should not only verify terms of contracts (e.g. terms of data use) against user-defined policies but also have mechanisms built in to ensure non-repudiation of entities who have accepted these digital contracts. Efforts such as the UMA initiative are beginning to bring better evidentiary proof and enforceability of contracts into technical protocol flows.[40]

- **Development of institutional controls for digital institutions**: Currently, a number of proposals for the creation of virtual currencies (e.g. BitCoin,[41] Ven[42]) have underlying systems with the potential to evolve into self-governing 'digital institutions'.[43] Such systems and the institutions that operate on them will necessitate the development of a new paradigm to understand aspects of institutional control within their context.

Scenarios of Use in Context

Developing frameworks for big data that effectively balance economic, legal, security, and other interests requires an understanding of the relevant context and applicable scenarios within which the data exists.

A sound starting point from which to establish the applicable scenarios of use is to enumerate the institutions involved with a given set of big data, and develop a description of how or why they hold, access, or otherwise intermediate the data. Although big data straddles multiple BLT boundaries, one or more institutions are typically able to, or in some situations required to, manage and control the data. The public good referred to in the introduction of this book can be articulated as design requirements or even as certification criteria applicable to those institutions that operate the systems through which the big data is computed or flows.

It may be also be necessary to narrowly define certain aspects of the scenario in which the data exist in order to establish the basic ownership, control, and other expectations of the key parties. For example, describing a transaction as a financial exchange may not provide enough relevant detail to reveal the rights, obligations, or other outcomes reasonably expected by the individuals and organizations involved. The sale of used cars via an app, the conduct of a counseling session via Google Hangout, and the earning of a master's degree via an online university all represent scenarios in which the use case of a financial exchange takes place. However, each of these scenarios occurs in a context that is easily identifiable: the sale of goods and deeper access to financial information if the car is financed; the practice of therapy by a licensed professional accessing and creating confidential mental health data; or e-learning services and protected educational records and possibly deeper financial information if the program is funded by scholarship or loans. The scenarios can also identify the key elements necessary to establish existing consumer rights – the people (a consumer and a used car dealer), the transaction (purchase of a used car), the data (sales and title data, finance information, etc.), and the systems (the third-party app and its relevant services or functions, state DMV services, credit card and bank services, etc.). The rights established by relevant state lemon laws, the Uniform Commercial Code, and other applicable rules will determine when duties arise or are terminated, what must be promised, what can be repudiated, by whom data must be kept secure, and other requirements or constraints on the use of personal data and big data. These and other factors differ when a transaction that seems identical operates within a different scenario, and even scenarios will differ depending on which contexts apply. The following four elements are critical for defining high-level goals and objectives:

1.   Who are the people in the scenario (e.g. who are the parties involved and what are their respective roles and relationships)?
2.   What are the relevant interactions (e.g. what transactions or other actions are conducted by or with the people involved)?
3.   What are the relevant data and datasets (e.g. what types of data are created, stored, computed, transmitted, modified, or deleted)?
4.   What are the relevant systems (e.g. what services or other software are used by the people, for the transactions, or with the data)?

Inspired by common law, the New Deal on Data sets out general principles of ownership that both guide and inform basic relationships and expectations. However, the dynamic bundle of recombinant rights and responsibilities constituting 'ownership' interests in personal data and expectations pertaining to big data vary significantly from context to context, and even from one scenario to another within a given general context. Institutional controls and other system safeguards are important methods to ensure that there are context-appropriate outcomes that are consistent with clearly applicable system scenarios as well as the contours and foundations for a greater public good. The New Deal on Data can be achieved in part by sets of institutional controls involving governance, business, legal, and technical aspects of big data and interoperating systems. Reference scenarios can be used to reveal signature features of the New Deal on Data in various contexts and can serve as anchors in evaluating what institutional controls are well aligned to achieve a balance of economic, privacy, and other interests.

The types of requirements and rules governing participation by individuals and organizations in trust networks vary depending on the facts and circumstances of the transactions, data types, relevant roles of people, and other factors. Antecedent but relevant networks such as credit card systems, trading partner systems, and exchange networks are instructive not only for their many common elements but also as important examples of how vastly different they are from one another in their contexts, scenarios, legal obligations, business models, technical processes, and other signature patterns. Trust networks that are formed to help manage big data in ways that appropriately respect personal data rights and other broader interests will similarly succeed to the extent they can tolerate or promote a wide degree of heterogeneity among participants for BLT matters that need not be uniform or directly harmonized. In some situations, new business models and contexts will emerge that require fresh thinking and novel combinations of roles or types of relationships among transacting parties. In these cases, understanding the actual context and scenarios is critical in customizing acceptable and sustainable BLT rules and systems. Example scenarios can describe deeper fact-based situations and circumstances in the context of social science research involving personal data and big data.[44] The roles of people, their interactions, the use of data, and the design of the corresponding systems reflect and support the New Deal on Data in ways that deliberately provide greater immediate value to stakeholders than is typically expected.

The New Deal on Data is designed to provide good value to anyone creating, using, or benefiting from personal data, but the vision need not be adopted in its entirety before its value becomes apparent. Its principles can be adopted on a large scale in increments – an economic sector, transaction type, or data type at a time. Adopting the New Deal on Data in successive phases helps to address typical objections to change based on cost, disruption, or overregulation. Policy incentives can further address these objections, for example by allowing safe harbor protections for organizations operating under the rules of a trust network.

Predesigned use cases can provide benchmarks for determining whether given uses of personal data are consistent with measurable criteria. Such criteria can be used to establish compliance with the rules of a trust network and for certification by government for the right to safe harbor or other protections. Because the New Deal on Data is rooted in common law and the social compact, the appropriate set of rights and expectations covering privacy and other personal data interests can be enumerated, debated, and agreed upon in ways that fit the given use cases.

Conclusions

Society today faces unprecedented challenges and meeting them will require access to personal data, so we can understand how society works, how we move around, what makes us productive, and how everything from ideas to diseases spread. The insights must be actionable and available in real time, thus engaging the population, creating the nervous system of the society. In this chapter we have reviewed how big data collected in institutional contexts can be used for the public good. In many cases, although the data needed to create a better society has already been collected, it sits in the closed silos of companies and governments. We have described how the silos can be opened using well-designed and carefully implemented sets of institutional controls, covering business, legal, and technical dimensions. The framework for doing this – the New Deal on Data – postulates that the primary driver of change must be recognizing that ownership of personal data rests with the people that data is about. This ownership – the right to use, transfer, and remove the data – ensures that the data is available for the public good, while at the same time protecting the privacy of citizens.

The New Deal on Data is still new. We have described here our efforts to understand the technical means of its implementation, the legal framework around it, its business ramifications, and the direct value of the greater access to data that it enables. It is clear that companies must play the major role in implementing the New Deal, incentivized by business opportunities, guided by legislation, and pressured by demands from users. Only with such orchestration will it be possible to modernize the current system of data ownership and put immense quantities and capabilities of collected personal data to good use.

See Appendix A for the WEF whitepaper on "Personal Data: The Emergence of a New Asset Class."

CHAPTER 5

The Rise of Decentralized Personal Data Markets

Jacopo Staiano, Guy Zyskind, Bruno Lepri,
Nuria Oliver, Alex Pentland

THE RISE OF DECENTRALIZED PERSONAL DATA MARKETS

The almost universal adoption of mobile phones, the exponential increase in the use of Internet services, social media platforms, and credit cards, and the proliferation of wearable devices and connected objects (Internet of Things) have resulted in a massive production of human behavioral data that characterize many aspects of daily life with extremely fine temporal and spatial granularities[9]. Such ubiquitous collection of personal data represents an invaluable resource for designing and building systems that are able to understand the needs and activities of both individuals and communities - so as to e.g. provide personalized, context-aware feedback and services[8]. Consequently, many public services of societal interest (e.g. city planning, public health, emergency response) could be greatly improved by the analysis of this data. Similarly, many commercial services, as Waze or recommendation engines, require personal data such as location, purchase, or browsing history.

This scenario, however, raises unprecedented privacy challenges and concerns derived from the collection, storage and usage of vast amounts of personal data[1&16]. At the same time, people are becoming more aware of the value and the risks associated with their personal data, most especially around location data[22]. This increased concern is reflected in new privacy regulations for mobile phone data (http://ec.europa.eu/justice/data-protection/individuals/index_en.htm) and in research studies and debates about the difficulty of anonymization for these sorts of data[11].

The core problem, then, is how can an individual share sensitive data for a public service (e.g. city planning) or a desired commercial service (e.g. traffic and driving advice) and be sure that the data will only be used for the intended purpose? This question implicitly recognizes the risks in terms not only of possible abuses in the usage of the personal data but also of the "missed chance for innovation" that is inherent to the current dominant paradigm of siloed data collection, management, and exploitation, which precludes participation to a wide range of actors, most notably the very producers of personal data (i.e. the users).

Recently, new user-centric models for personal data management have been proposed, in order to empower individuals with more control of their own data's life-cycle[14]. To this end, researchers and companies are developing repositories which implement medium-grained access control to different kinds of personally identifiable information (PII), such as e.g. passwords, social security numbers and health data[23], location[10,12] and personal data collected by means of smartphones or connected devices[12].

Previous work has also introduced the concept of personal data markets in which individuals sell their own personal data to entities interested in buying it[2]. While personal data markets might be the next natural step in designing technology to support a transparent and privacy-preserving use of personal data, they are still at a research stage due to a number of technological and regulatory challenges. In order to implement a market, it is necessary to connect potential buyers (demand) with sellers (offer) and provide a trustworthy mechanism for the exchange of goods or value between buyers and sellers. In a personal data market, the sellers are individuals (who own their personal data), the buyers are corporations, researchers, governments, etc., and the mechanism for the exchange of "goods" is still to be defined.

Moreover, research works have consistently found that technology users are increasingly concerned about their privacy related to personal data sharing[16,22]. In order to realize the vision of personal data markets, we believe that humans should be placed at the center. Hence, beyond technological implementations of enabling platforms, it is of paramount importance to carry out user-centric studies to shed light on human factors related to personal data markets, such as personal preferences, sensitivities and valuations of personal data.

In a recent study[19] we investigated, in a living lab setting[5], the monetary value that people assign to different kinds of personal data as collected by their mobile phone, including location and communication information. Five major insights related to how our participants valued their mobile personal data emerged:

1.   ***Bulk mobile personal information is perceived as most valuable***, when compared to individual mobile personal data points (e.g. the collection of all locations collected throughout the study was considered to be more valuable than a single location). Interestingly, the values obtained during our study are found to be lower that those reported in a similar study, which focused on the valuation of personal web-browsing information[4].

2.   ***Location, location, location!*** We observed the highest valuation to be consistently associated with location information, which

also emerged as the most opted-out category of mobile PII. Several participants also expressed that they did not want to be geolocalized and considered location information to be highly sensitive and personal. Moreover, we found statistically significant correlations between mobility behaviors (e.g. mean daily distance traveled, daily radius of gyration, etc.) and valuations of personal data. Not all users value their personal data equally: the more someone travels on a daily basis, the more s/he values not only her/his location information but also her/his communication and application usage information. These insights may have an impact on the design of commercial location-sharing applications. While users of such applications might consent at install time to share their location with the app, our work suggests that when explicitly asked about either individual or bulk location data, 17% of users decide not to share their location information. In addition, mobility behaviors will influence the valuations of PII. Tsai et al.[21] conducted an online survey with more than 500 American subjects to evaluate their own perceptions of the likelihood of several location-sharing scenarios along with the magnitude of the benefit or harm of each scenario (e.g. being stalked or finding people in an emergency). The majority of the participants found the risks of using location-sharing technologies to be higher than the benefits. However, today a significant number of very popular mobile apps such as Foursquare and Facebook Places make use of location data. These popular commercial location sharing apps seem to mitigate its users' privacy concerns by allowing them to selectively report their location using check-in funtionalities instead of tracking them automatically.

3.   ***Socio-demographic characteristics do not dictate value,
     behavior does***. When we correlated bid values against socio-
     demographic characteristics of the participants in our study,
     we did not find any significant correlations. On the other
     hand, we found statistically significant correlations between
     behavior (particularly mobility and app usage) and valuations
     of bids. From our findings it seems that personal differences
     in valuations of mobile PII are associated with behavioral
     differences rather than demographic differences. In particular,
     the larger the daily distance traveled and radius of gyration,
     the higher the valuation of PII. Conversely, the more apps a
     person used, the lower the valuation of PII. A potential reason
     for this correlation is due to the fact that savvy app users have
     accepted that mobile apps collect their mobile PII in order to
     provide their service and hence consider their mobile PII to be
     less valuable.

4.   ***Trust yourself, not the government!*** From both our study and
     Carrascal et al.[4], it clearly emerges that individuals mainly trust
     themselves to handle their own personal data. Despite this
     finding, note that most users today do not have the tools to
     be able to handle their personal data in a secure, transparent
     and user-friendly way. This result supports the adoption of a
     decentralized and user-centric architecture for personal data
     management.

5.   ***Unusual days lead to higher bids***. While analyzing the data
     collected during our study, we noticed that the bids -in all
     categories- for two specific days were significantly higher than
     for the rest of the days. One of these highly valued days was a

holiday and the other was characterised by extremely strong winds causing multiple road blocks and incidents. This suggests that not all personal data, even within the same category and level of complexity, is valued equally by our participants. This finding has a direct implication for personal data markets and for services that monetize mobile personal data.

To sum up, our findings show how (1) location, behavioral and bulk PII are the most sensitive and valued types of personal data; and (2) users manifest a desire to control both access and usage of their personal data. These results highlight privacy concerns that individuals have shown in real-world experiments.

On this topic, Orange commissioned an independent research agency, Loadhouse, to conduct 2028 online interviews of mobile phone users in UK, France, Spain, and Poland to understand consumer attitudes related to personal data usage[25]. The goal was to uncover the extent and nature of trust between consumers and a variety of service providers, what value consumers assign to their personal data and the factors that influence this value. Interestingly, European consumers seem to struggle for have control over their own personal data while companies are becoming more sophisticated in capturing and using these data. In addition, the results of the study show that customers understand that their own data has value to businesses and this value is variable based on the type of information and the relationship with the organisation. More specifically, there are three types of data that customers identify when it comes to their willingness to share their data with an organisation: (i) data related to friends and other contacts or data related to private information (such as their income), (ii) behavioural data, including information such as location or mobile purchase history, and (iii) basic demographic data, such as name, date of birth, mobile number or marital status.

While these research works support the creation of a personal data market from a user-centric perspective, it also uncover a key technological challenge that still would need to be addressed in order to realize such a personal data market: a method for secure data sharing that would guarantee both data privacy and data integrity. Combined with a lack of existing tools to securely enable personal data markets, such findings led us to develop ENIGMA, a computational framework that addresses these privacy concerns while enabling applications of both commercial and societal interest to leverage personal information in a trusted manner. In the next section we describe ENIGMA and illustrate how it could be used to implement a personal data market.

ENIGMA: A decentralized platform for secure personal data sharing

As we discussed in Chapter 3, ENIGMA is a decentralized platform that uses at its core a blockchain protocol to enable secure data sharing such that it removes the need for a trusted third party and enables the autonomous control of personal data[26]. Given the properties of blockchain, Enigma users are able for the first time to share and sell their personal data with cryptographic guarantees regarding their privacy.

ENIGMA leverages the recent technological trend of decentralization: advances in the fields of cryptography and decentralized computer networks have resulted in the emergence of a novel technology –

known as the blockchain – which has the potential to reduce the role of one of the most important actors in our society – the middle man[3,7]. By allowing people to transfer a unique piece of digital property or data to others, in a safe, secure, and immutable way, this technology can create digital currencies (e.g., bitcoin) that are not backed by any governmental body[13]; self-enforcing digital contracts, called smart contracts, whose execution does not require any human intervention (e.g., Ethereum)[20]; and decentralized marketplaces that aim to operate free from regulations[7]. Hence, ENIGMA tackles the challenge of providing a secure and trustworthy mechanism for the exchange of goods in a personal data market.

In a personal data market scenario, buyers are likely to be companies, public institutions and researchers, while sellers are individuals who receive compensation for sharing their own data.
The ENIGMA system allows any type of computation to be outsourced to the cloud while guaranteeing the privacy of the underlying data and the correctness of the result. A core feature in the system is that it allows the data owners to define and control who can query it, thus ensuring that the approved parties only learn the output. Moreover, no data leaks in the process to any other party.

ENIGMA itself is comprised of a network of computers that store and execute queries. Using secure multi-party computation (sMPC or MPC), each computer only sees random pieces of the data, a fact that prevents information leaks. Furthemore, queries carry a micro-payment for the computing resources as well as to those users whose data is queried, thus providing the foundation for the rise of a data market.

When owners share data, the data is split into several random pieces called shares. Shares are created in a process of secret-sharing[18] and perfectly hide the underlying data while maintaining some necessary properties allowing them to later be queried in this masked form. Since users in ENIGMA are owners of their data, we need a trusted database to publicly store a proof of who owns which data. ENIGMA makes use of a blockchain as a decentralized secure database that is not owned by any party. Our solution is based on Zyskind et al.[24,26,] which also allows an owner to designate which services can access its data and under what conditions. This way, when a service requests a computation, parties can query the blockchain and ensure that it holds the appropriate permissions. In addition to being a secure and distributed public database, the blockchain is also used to facilitate payments from services to computing parties and owners, while enforcing correct permissions and verifying that queries execute correctly.

In the context of a secure market for personal mobile data, ENIGMA serves as the underlying enabling technology for selling and buying personal data. The owners of the data would have access to an interface where they could select which mobile personal data (automatically collected by their mobile phones) would be uploaded into the system and which services could issue queries against their data. In exchange for enabling their personal data to be used by services, the owners would be digitally reimbursed. Their raw data would never be exposed or seen by any service or user.

The ENIGMA system offers owners not only full control of the personal data but also transparency on which services are accessing their data and for which purposes. Service providers would be able to monetize the personal data available in the system without ever having access to the raw data. They would have to pay the owners of the data a fair price which would be proportional to the value that such data brings to their business. Finally, thanks to ENIGMA's blockchain technology all transactions would take place while preserving data-integrity and privacy.

Conclusion

Current transformations of the "data ecology" are substantially due to the exponential growth of mobile and ubiquitous computing, together with big data analysis. These shifts are undeniably having a dramatic impact on people's personal data sharing awareness, sensitivities and desires. The first wave of social media, geo-social, and Web 2.0 applications have exploited personal data as a market opportunity with little participation by the producers of the data: the end users. However, today we have reached critical mass in privacy concerns and awareness on the use of personal data, partially due to media exposure of breaches and intelligence scandals. This critical mass is increasingly demanding "a new deal on data"[15] where transparency, control and privacy are at the core of any data-driven service.

The surge of connected sensors in both private and public spaces is expected to further exacerbate this tension, hence potentially limiting both the business and societal impact that the next-generation of data-driven applications could have, for instance in smart city scenarios. A multi-disciplinary effort, comprising sociologists, lawyers, technologists and policy-makers is therefore needed to address the problem of personal data access and control. A user-centric Personal Data Market approach, coupled with cryptographic guarantees on data access and usage, as presented in this article, represents a possible answer to resolving such tension, which we plan to empirically validate in the future.

We envision a world where technology serves as a mean both to business innovation and societal progress, rather than an obstacle or a tool for undermining people and ultimately democracies: mindful citizens, supported by technology that respects their rights and fulfills their needs, are in our vision key to build the smart and data-driven societies of tomorrow.

CHAPTER 6

Enabling Humanitarian Use of Mobile Phone Data

Yves-Alexandre de Montjoye, Jake Kendall,
Cameron F. Kerry

Mobile phones are now ubiquitous in developing countries, with 89 active subscriptions per 100 inhabitants.[1] Though many types of population data are scarce in developing countries, the metadata generated by millions of mobile phones and recorded by mobile phone operators can enable unprecedented insights about individuals and societies. Used with appropriate restraint, this data has great potential for good, including immediate use in the fight against Ebola.[2]

To operate their networks, mobile phone operators collect call detail records—metadata of who called whom, at what time, and from where. After the removal of names, phone numbers, or other obvious identifiers, this data can be shared with researchers to reconstruct precise country-scale mobility patterns and social graphs. These data have already been used to study importation routes of infectious diseases,[3] migration patterns, or economic transactions.[4] Such data is now being actively sought to inform the fight against Ebola[5] but, despite the promise, this effort appears stalled.[6]

As part of our research at MIT, we examined two operational use cases of mobile phone data for development modeled on previous research. The first case, involved the use of location metadata to understand and quantify the spread of infectious diseases (e.g. malaria or Ebola) within and among countries.[6] The second case considered the use of behavioral indicators derived from mobile phone metadata to micro-target outreach or drive uptake of agricultural technologies or health seeking behavior.[7] Here, mobile phone data could be used to define subgroups based on specific traits and behaviors, which would then receive messages or other outreach from the mobile operator.[8] We also considered cases where the data could be used to select individuals to be identified and contacted directly in limited circumstances. These two scenarios are quite distinct from a regulatory and privacy perspective, as we discuss below.

These mobile phone data case studies revealed ways in which, despite the promise, regulatory barriers and privacy challenges are preventing the use of mobile phone metadata from realizing its full potential. More specifically, our analysis showed (1) the lack of commonly- accepted practices for sharing mobile phone data in privacy-conscientious ways and (2) an uncertain and country-specific regulatory landscape for data-sharing especially for cross- border data sharing.

While some forward-looking companies have been sharing limited data with researchers in privacy-conscientious ways, these barriers and challenges are making it unnecessarily hard for carriers to share data for humanitarian purposes.[9-10] We describe these issues further and offer recommendations moving forward.

Protecting the Identity of Subjects

Mobile phone metadata made available to researchers should never include names, home addresses, phone numbers, or other obvious identifiers. Indeed, many regulations and data sharing agreements rely heavily on protecting anonymity by focusing on a predefined list of personally-identifiable information that should not be shared. In the United States, for example, the privacy rule issued by the Department of Health and Human Services to protect the privacy of patient health records specifies[18] different types of data about patients that must be removed from datasets for them to be considered de-identified.[11]

However, elimination of specific identifiers is not enough to prevent re-identification. The anonymity of such datasets has been compromised before and research[12] shows that, in mobile phone datasets, knowing as few as four data points—approximate places and times where an individual was when they made a call or send a text— is enough to re-identify 95% of people in a given dataset. In general, there will be very few people who are in the same place at the same time on four different occasions, which creates a unique "signature" for the individual making it easy to isolate them as unique in the dataset. The same research also used unicity to shows that simply anonymized mobile phone datasets provide little anonymity even when coarsened or noised.

This means that removing identifying information makes isolating and identifying a specific person in the dataset only slightly more challenging because that person can be identified using available sources of data that link location with a name or another identifier (e.g. geo-tagged posts on social media, travel schedules, etc.). Wholesale re-identification is more difficult, however, because re-identification of a large fraction of the dataset requires access to a full list of people and places they have been, which may not be as easy to acquire. Nevertheless, a determined attacker can still re-identify people using such data. Therefore, removing personally identifiable information is only a first step in most instances and more stringent approaches are required unless trust in the recipient of a dataset is high.

Recognizing the limits of an approach to anonymity and re-identification that focuses only on identity information like names or ID numbers, governments have sought to expand protection beyond identity to any information that can be used to identify an individual. In 2007, the federal Office of Management and Budget added to its list of identifiers "any other personal information which is linked or linkable to an individual."[13] In Europe, the Directive 95/46/EC cautions that "account should be taken of all the means likely to be used" to identify an individual,[14] and a thorough recent opinion of EU privacy regulators provided technical guidance on the challenges and risks of re-identification.[15]

The challenge of these broad definitions is that they are open-ended. No existing anonymization methods or protocols can guarantee at 100 percent that mobile phone metadata cannot be re-identified unless the data has been greatly modified or aggregated. Hence, open-ended requirements can be unverifiable and, taken to their logical extreme, so strict as to prohibit any sharing of data even when risk of re-identification is very limited.

We believe this places too much emphasis on a limited risk of re-identification and unclear harm without considering the social benefits of using this data such as better managing outbreaks or informing government response after a disaster.[16] Special consideration should be given to cases where the data will be used for significant public good or to avoid serious harm to people. Furthermore, data sharing should allow for greater levels of disclosure to highly trusted data recipients with strong processes, data security, audit, and access control mechanisms in place. For example, trusted third parties at research universities might warrant access to richer, less anonymized data for research purposes and be relied on not to try to re-identify individuals or to use the data inappropriately.

For both use cases, we defined data-sharing protocols that would allow for the intended analysis, while protecting privacy. We contemplate releasing anonymized data to research teams and NGOs in a form that adds technical difficulty to re-identification, limits the amount of data that would be re-identified, and further limiting the risk of re-identification or abuse with a legal agreement that specifies that only specific purposes and other protocols can be applied to the data. In our analysis, we focused on a middle ground scenario of relatively open sharing of data with multiple research teams and/or NGOs, with some (but limited) accountability and auditability. We did not consider a fully-public release where a very high level of anonymization would be required, nor a release to a highly trusted third party with strong data protection in place that might allow weakly-anonymized data sharing.

For our first use case, we concluded that a 5 percent sampling of the data on a monthly basis, resampled with new identifiers every month for a year and coarsened temporally and spatially into 12-hour periods (7 a.m. to 7 p.m.) and by regions within countries would be the right balance between utility and privacy.[17] It would adequately show individuals' mobility across regions under study and the number of nights spent in infected regions while providing significant—but not absolute—protection of identity and limiting the amount of data that would be re-identified.

For our second use case, we concluded that the behavioral indicators[18] derived from metadata can be shared with the researchers safely, provided outliers have been removed. Researchers could then use this data to segment the population into specific sub-groups based on traits like calling patterns, mobility, number of contacts, etc. People fitting these criteria could then be contacted by the mobile phone operators through text messages or other communications. Their phone numbers would be known only to the mobile phone operators.

We also considered cases where specific individuals could be contacted based on criteria applied to the data. To do so would require either (a) including in the dataset pseudonymous—but unique— identifiers that make it possible to connect data showing certain traits (such as a likely exposure to disease based on travel patterns) with specific individuals, or (b) including telephone numbers in the dataset so that researchers and/or NGOs can contact the individuals identified directly. Because it enables re-identification, the former would be a departure from good privacy practices unless the data was recipient highly trusted, and the second would be a clear departure because it disclosed unmodified personally identifiable information.

Nevertheless, re-identification could be vital in case of emergencies such as an earthquake.[19] These alternate use cases illustrate further the need to develop mechanisms for trusted third parties to maintain data under strong controls for use, access, security, and accountability.[20]

More generally, promising computational privacy approaches to make the re-identification of mobile phone metadata harder include sampling the data, making the antenna GPS coordinates less precise through voronoi translation for example,[21] or limiting the longitudinality of the data to cover shorter periods of time. These could go as far as to set up systems or collaborations where researchers could pose questions of the data, but where mobile operators would only share with researchers "answers,"[22] such as behavioral indicators or summary statistics.[23] Each of these alternatives could be employed depending on the use the data is put to, the amount and sensitivity of the data that would be uncovered, how and by whom the data will be governed and housed, and the attendant risks of harm.

Engaging Government Support

The second challenge we identified to humanitarian use of mobile phone metadata is an uncertain and country- specific regulatory landscape for data-sharing. Our study focused on Africa, where data privacy regulation has been evolving along two lines. The Francophone countries—mostly located in West Africa, where current exposure to Ebola is greatest—have tended to adopt privacy frameworks modeled on the 1995 European Privacy Directive and supervised by national data protection authorities. Meanwhile English-speaking countries with common law systems either have not yet adopted comprehensive privacy laws, or have adopted country-specific laws.

This landscape presents a number of barriers to humanitarian use of mobile phone metadata.

First, legal uncertainty complicates the design of data-sharing protocols. Indeed, even in countries that have had laws and regulatory agencies in place for some time, the relevant rules have not developed in enough detail to address an issue that is often uncertain even in the most developed legal systems.

Second, as discussed above, questions about the validity of most methods of de-identification persist particularly in countries that use open-ended definitions of anonymization such as the EU one. There exists no widely accepted data-sharing standards to help various actors achieve a rational privacy/utility tradeoff in using mobile phone metadata.

Third, regardless of legal systems, compatible data-sharing protocols—including data de-identification—have to be designed and validated on a country by country basis. For example, data-sharing protocols have to be compatible, which includes having both the phone number and the mobile phone identifier[24] hashed with the same function and salt[25] to allow for mobile phones to be followed across border, even if the user changes SIM cards. These issues make cross-border data sharing or intra-regional tracking of population flows particularly complex and costly. Yet such cross-country sharing is essential in the fight against diseases such as malaria or the current Ebola outbreak.[26]

Fourth, our second use case contemplated that, in general, only behavioral indicators derived from carriers' metadata would be shared with researchers but that, in specific and limited circumstances where these indicators show an individual would benefit from intervention, the identity could be used to enable remote intervention such as targeted texts sent by the operator, or identification through mechanisms that carefully control the release and use of this information.

In the absence of explicit consent from users to such disclosure and use of data from their mobile phones, these forms of re-identification of data subjects presents obvious privacy challenges and may come into conflict with most privacy legal regimes absent specific exceptions. The EU Privacy Directive provides that data processing must have a lawful basis, but that such a basis may be "to protect the vital interests of the data subject," or "in the public interest, or in the exercise of official authority, and recognizes "public health" as such a public interest."[27] Thus, it will take the support of national governments, their health ministries, and their data protection authorities to enable use of data especially in such exigent situations, but also for a range of humanitarian applications.[28]

Conclusion: Roadmaps Needed

These privacy challenges and regulatory barriers are making humanitarian data-sharing much harder than it should be for mobile phone operators and are significantly limiting greater use of mobile phone metadata in development or aid programs and in research areas like computational social science, development economics, and public health.

To realize the potential of this data for social good, we recommend the following:

1.   There is a clear need for companies, NGOs, researchers, privacy experts, and governments to agree on a set of best practices for new privacy-conscientious metadata sharing models in different development use cases—a wider and higher-level discussion of the kind our MIT working group conducted. These best practices would help carriers and policymakers strike the right balance between privacy and utility in the use of metadata and could be instantiated by data-protection agencies, institutional review boards, and in data protection laws and policies. This would make it easier and less risky for carriers to support humanitarian and research uses of this data, and for

researchers and NGOs to use these metadata appropriately.

2. Such best practices should accept that there are no perfect ways to de-identify data—and probably will never be.[29] There will always be some risk that must be balanced against the public good that can be achieved. While much more research is needed in computational privacy, widespread adoption of existing techniques as standards could enable this trend of sharing data in a privacy- conscientious way.

3. Standards and practices as well as legal regulation also need to address and incorporate trust mechanisms for humanitarian sharing of data in a more nuanced way. Protection of individual privacy includes not only protection against re-identification, but also data security and protection against unwanted uses of data. Risk of re-identification is not a purely theoretical concept nor is it binary and it should be assessed vis-à-vis the level of trust placed in the data recipient and the strength of their systems and processes. Tracking of migration patterns or analysis of behavior patterns may offer enormous benefits for disease prevention and treatment, but it is possible to envision more malignant uses by actors ranging from disgruntled employees of the data recipient to authoritarian governments. The recognition of trusted third-parties and systems to manage datasets, enable detailed audits, and control the use of data could enable greater sharing of these data among multiple parties while providing a barrier against risks.

There is a need for governments to focus on adopting laws and rules that simplify the collection and use of mobile phone metadata for research and public good purposes. Governments should also seek to harmonize laws on the sharing of metadata with common identifiers across national borders. The African Union took what could be a step in this direction last June, when it approved the African Convention on Cyber Security and Personal Data Protection seeking to advance Africa's digital agenda and harmonize rules among African nations.[30] The treaty, which will not take effect until adopted by 15 member states, commits members to adopting a legal framework that follows the template of the European Privacy Directive. Clear and consistent rules will help but only provided they take a pragmatic and privacy-conscientious approach to anonymization, cross-border transfers, and novel uses that enable public good uses of data and allow for public health emergencies and other valuable research.

Research based on mobile phone data, computational privacy, and data protection rules all may seem secondary when confronted by the challenges of poverty, disease, and basic economic growth. But they are on the critical path to realizing the great potential of information technology to help address these critical problems.

CHAPTER 7

Living Labs for Trusted Data

David Shrier, Alex Pentland

We have discussed the imperatives for a better data and trust architecture, the methods for delivering one, and some of the privacy and private market implications associated with new methods of data governance and societal interplay. How can we be assured that the theories developed in the lab, in conferences and workshops, and in simulation systems, correlate to actual behavior in real-world settings? How do we produce quantifiable, repeatable results and systems that scale to the level of a country? What are ways we can explore the potential of these new systems to improve society?

Over decades of experimentation, we have found that "Living Labs" generate society-scale results that can be examined, debated, approved, and ultimately replicated across domains as diverse as health, crime prevention, and transportation. We can also guide corporate innovation and innovation and culture change, for Living Labs can apply equally to corporate settings as well as civic and community. We will now discuss how this platform can build scalable solutions to problems faced by people worldwide.

Introduction

Living Labs are unique, new type of field research platform that translates big data analysis into action, generating new insights by quantifying real world interactions and delivering interventions that change behavior at scale.

For each Lab, we typically construct a team of 12 to 16 researchers, leveraging new technologies and data infrastructure, to investigate and deploy interventions against societal problems. We apply unique software and hardware platforms developed at MIT for big data analysis of social patterns in real environments, in order to uncover actionable insights into human behavior. We then use our data platform to leverage these insights to effect change and provide results during the project.

Our Living Labs are highly collaborative efforts that typically involve regional universities, government, corporate, and nonprofit entities, in order to maximize the benefits delivered by the program by ensuring compatibility with local conditions and promoting effective knowledge transfer.

Labs currently extant or in development include the Principality of Andorra, Trento, Italy; Luxembourg; Bogota, Colombia; and Mexico City, Mexico.

Funding can come from a combination of corporate, governmental and private sources, to support a Living Lab with a duration of typically 2 to 5 years (although our Lab in Trento just renewed for another 3 year term). An additional, and typical greater, amount is normally invested to build local capacity, since once solution paths are uncovered, the scale-up is taken on by local partners rather than our research team.

Focus Parameters

Living Labs are typically set up in a particular city, province or district in order to maximize impact while minimizing cost. In a corporate setting they may be established initially at a single work site, although we currently are developing research streams around remote workers and multi-site collaborative environments.

For civic Living Labs, we typically look at governmental regions (whether cities, districts or states) that have the folllowing

characteristics:
* population of 2 million to 20 million;
* viable economic foundation.
* progressive government with a desire to drive growth; and
* strong university or other local partners for us to collaborate with.

In a corporate setting, we would normally seek:
* deployment into more than 100 employees (although initially may start with a work group or department)
* clear identification of a problem space (innovation, efficiency, health of the worker, intergeneration communication and knowledge transfer, etc.)
* stakeholders in both line operating roles as well as administrative functions such as HR

Scoping Process

MIT engages in a scoping and design process with its stakeholders when developing a Living Lab. Examples of solution-spaces that we can pursue in civic engagement include:
* Understanding and improving public health
* Optimizing transportation systems
* Financial inclusion and financial access
* Systems to prepare for, detect, and address contingencies such as floods, epidemics (H1N1 outbreak), etc.
* Enhancing innovation to support economic development
* Reducing crime

Examples of corporate solutions spaces:
* Improving workflow efficiency
* Enhancing collaboration within groups and across groups

- Decoding behaviors of highly successful archetypes (i.e., the "ideal researcher", the "ideal sales person", etc.) and development of assessment methods to assist with recruiting and onboarding
- Optimizing creativity and innovation

Examples of Living Labs

Below are examples that illustrate the span and scope of Living Labs we have deployed or are currently deploying:

Dimension	Description
Energy Consumption	We used data analytics and a unique set of social incentives, in collaboration with a private sector partner, to reduce energy utilization by over 17% in a Swiss Canton. This enabled the Canton to use all-hydroelectric power instead of needing to activate diesel generators. The behavior-change was equivalent to what would normally be achieved with a 100% price increase.[1]

Financial Services	Employing transaction data extracted from a bank's own customers in Europe, we were able to demonstrate an improvement to credit modeling for behaviors such as late payment, over limit, or credit default that were 30% to 49% better than traditional demographic models. This holds the promise of not only helping the bank better manage its existing customer base, but even to extend credit to the unbanked or underbanked (over 2 billion people worldwide lack bank accounts).[2]
Health	Working with the telecom Orange, we organized the first Data Commons for the D4D Challenge in conjunction with the United Nations and the World Economic Forum. Convening 86 research teams from around the world, we analyzed a large phone data set for the largest city in a West African country and determined how to reduce the spread of infectious disease by 20% through placement of health clinics and timing of vaccinations. 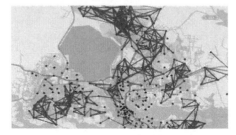

Crime	Using a combination of geospatial data from telecom O2 and government statistics, we were able to build a predictive model that illustrated in London that, by redeploying existing police personnel into areas predicted to have high incidence of crime, you could substantially reduce crime rates. We were told that this technique was used in Latin America in a major city to reduce crime...by 70%. 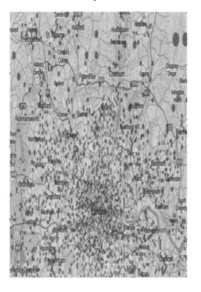

Tourism	Andorra is a tiny country in the Pyrenees bordered by France to the north and Spain to the south. With approximately 80,000 citizens, the country sees as many as 12 million tourists annually. Changing dynamics of its tourism industry have prompted the government and the local businesses to form a non-profit to collaborate with MIT around re-architecting the national economy to make it more vibrant and innovative, focused on improving the tourism experience.

Young Families	In Trento, an autonomous part of Italy, our Living Lab (sponsored by Telecom Italia, Telefonica, the local Cooperative, and local government) enrolled more than 100 young families for 3 years, measuring social interactions, mobility routines, spending patterns, surveys, etc. From this data came practical systems that allowed these young families to improve their lives by predicting daily stress and mood, spending habits, etc. and providing relevant feedback. This Living Lab also developed new models for managing and sharing data, and explored the idea of personal data markets where subjects can sell their own data 

Corporate Culture Change	In two different large (> 100,000 employee) corporations in different industries (aerospace and telecommunications), we are helping management address profound and company-wide culture change issues. Instrumenting teams of workers, we are identifying common behavioral characteristics and seeking to bridge different communications styles, workgroup organization, and shift behaviors at scale to transform their culture and create more nimble, entrepreneurial organizations.
Teamwork (and Education)	Using our online classroom into 95 countries, we are studying the dynamics of over 1,000 teams of business people working on innovation/entrepreneurship projects, to see how distance groups of typically half a dozen people can be enhanced to perform more like in-person teams around a month-long project deliverable (creation of a business plan for a new venture). We are also exploring aspects of peer learning and mentorship in a distance learning environment.

Unique Data-Driven Approach

MIT Connection Science benefits from having proven software, legal, and management tools for instrumenting, understanding, and changing user behavior.

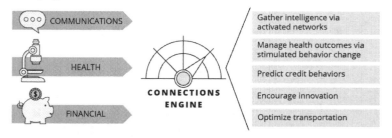

Setting up a Living Lab begins with an initial data and systems audit conducted by MIT researchers in order to outline what capabilities are present and which will need to be created, in the given environment in which we are forming the Living Lab. Comprehensive data will then be fed into a pooled data commons. Implementation of MIT's OPAL/ENIGMA privacy and personal data protection systems (an open-source platform developed by Professor Pentland and collaborators), along with other best practices, can provide security and robustness, and protect user privacy while unleashing innovation.

Data analytics will be built, in part, around our Bandicoot library (bandicoot.mit.edu) of over 100 tools for mobile-derived behavioral analytics and visualization, providing a high degree of efficiency for deployment of

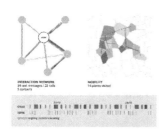

effective interventions.

Bandicoot-derived and other data are normalized, cross-linked, and integrated into a Connections Engine for deployment against select interventions.

 We have recently begun the Rhythm project (http://rhythm. mit.edu) which takes social physics methodology and deploys it into remote communications platforms like video chat and text channels, in harmony with in-person sociometric sensing from a new generation of sociometric badges. This platform holds the promise of enabling us to sense the full spectrum of communication within a typical corporate workplace, where in-person and remote meetings are everyday occurrences and sometimes blended experiences (with some participants remote and some in person).

Over time, as the OPAL/ENIGMA system is developed, we anticipate using this as the central data management platform for our Living Labs.

Data Privacy & Security. MIT is a world leader in protection of personal data and personal data privacy standards, and can help implement best-in-class methodologies and governance policies for personal data protection (likely with the OPAL/ENIGMA standard at the center of a solution). To further our work with data privacy & security, MIT has formed the Internet Trust Consortium (trust.mit.

edu), which provides core tools for our living labs. Chapters 2, 3, 4 and 5 talk more about this work.

Telecom Data. As we discussed in Chapter 4, we often use telecom data. The most essential elements are typically mobile data including call record (which number called which number, at what time) and location data, which can be abstracted inside the telecommunications company into "metadata" for subsequent analysis by MIT (i.e., no personally identifiable information leaves the telecom company).

For a given solution space, specific data sources may be needed or helpful, like economic growth data. MIT can make intelligent guesses using telecoms data even if certain other information is not available; for example, by overlaying telecoms positional signals on Google Maps, and look at rate of change of location, it is possible to make a reasonable guess if someone is in a car or on foot.

MIT Connection Science has long-standing relationships with a number of incumbent telecommunications companies around the world who can facilitate opening discussions for Living Lab collaboration in a given geography.   We have also we have successfully conducted Living Labs using other data sources, such as a bank's own payments data for our credit analytics projects. This is especially effective in countries where payments data is geo-located.

Data Commons Benefits. The use of pervasive technologies as a proxy to for more expensive traditional survey methods is of a particular interest as such methods can provide quick insights and understanding of social patterns, supply, and demand. Our Living Labs not only cover a larger sample of the population but also are also immune to some of the biases of surveys and have much higher time and space resolutions enabling better understanding at unprecedented scales. Another key advantage of the analysis of data gathered from pervasive technologies such as mobile phones is the very short time required to conduct a study. In contrast, conducting surveys requires a period of months if not years, and is often prohibitively expensive.

Activating Social Organizations

Living Labs have a life beyond the experimental period. Through exploration of a portfolio of societal interventions, we identify scalable solutions to critical issues. But what happens next? That's when private and public interests take over, expanding the initial interventions into repeatable, sustainable "social utilities" that scale up in domains such as health, transportation, financial, safety/crime and economic development. The sensing platform crafted in the initial Living Lab can be maintained and extended for continuous innovation.

Building a Better Tomorrow

MIT's mission is to solve humanity's greatest challenges, particularly via advancing the frontier of human knowledge and training the next generation of leaders to fulfill this promise. Living Labs support both the theory and practice of innovation, and so are central to achieving these goals. Living Lab initiatives align closely with MIT's mission by enhancing our understanding of human behavior at scale, especially with reference to social groupings, and provide a means of having positive impact on the world.

In building Living Labs, we draw on anti-disciplinary expertise across several of MIT's schools (Engineering, Management, Science, and Architecture & Planning / MIT Media Lab), as well as with our research collaborators from dozens of universities around the world.

We are by no means the only researchers using the Living Lab methodology. With more and more Living Labs proliferating around the world, we see our role as one of providing tools and insights that can be used globally to improve the human experience.

We continue to seek out new partners who can help us on the journey of exploration of the potential of Living Labs. We hope to transform societies and help companies to better engage their stakeholders. To make this possible, we need the Trust::Data framework described in this book, and advocates and evangelists who raise awareness of, and enhance the capabilities of, these powerful new tools. Please join us in building this better world

APPENDIX A

Personal Data:
The Emergence of a
New Asset Class

World Economic Forum

ACKNOWLEDGEMENTS

This document was prepared by the World Economic Forum, in partnership with the individuals and organisations listed below.

WORLD ECONOMIC FORUM

Professor Klaus Schwab	Executive Chairman
Alan Marcus	Senior Director, IT & Telecommunications Industries
Justin Rico Oyola	Associate Director and Project Lead, Telecommunications Industry
William Hoffman	Head, Telecommunications Industry

BAIN & COMPANY, INC.

Michele Luzi   Director

The following experts contributed substantial research and interviews throughout the "Rethinking Personal Data" project. We extend our sincere gratitude to all of them.

Julius Akinyemi	MIT
Alberto Calero	France Telecom
Ron Carpinella	Equifax
Chris Conley	ACLU
Douglas Dabérius	Nokia Siemens Networks
Timothy Edgar	Office of the Director of National Intelligence, USA
Jamie Ferguson	Kaiser Permanente

Michael Fertik	Reputation.com & Heroic Ventures
Tal Givoly	Amdocs
Kaliya Hamlin	Personal Data Ecosystem
William Heath	Mydex
Trevor Hughes	International Association of Privacy Professionals
Betsy Masiello	Google
Mita Mitra	BT Group
Drummond Reed	Information Card Foundation
Nasrin Rezai	Cisco
Natsuhiko Sakimura	OpenID Foundation
Kevin Stanton	MasterCard Advisors
Pamela Warren	McAfee
Von Wright	AT&T

PROJECT STEERING BOARD

This work would also not have been possible without the commitment of:

John Clippinger	Berkman Center for Internet and Society, Harvard University
Scott David	K&L Gates
Marc Davis	Microsoft
Robert Fabricant	frog design
Philip Laidler	STL Partners
Alex Pentland	MIT
Fabio Sergio	frog design
Simon Torrance	STL Partners

INTRODUCTION

We are moving towards a "Web of the world" in which mobile communications, social technologies and sensors are connecting people, the Internet and the physical world into one interconnected network.[1] Data records are collected on who we are, who we know, where we are, where we have been and where we plan to go. Mining and analysing this data give us the ability to understand and even predict where humans focus their attention and activity at the individual, group and global level.

"Personal data is the new oil of the Internet and the new currency of the digital world."
- Meglena Kuneva, European Consumer Commissioner, March 2009

This **personal data** – digital data created by and about people – is generating a new wave of opportunity for economic and societal value creation. The types, quantity and value of personal data being collected are vast: our profiles and demographic data from bank accounts to medical records to employment data. Our Web searches and sites visited, including our likes and dislikes and purchase histories. Our tweets, texts, emails, phone calls, photos and videos as well as the coordinates of our real-world locations. The list continues to grow. Firms collect and use this data to support individualised service-delivery business models that can be monetised. Governments employ personal data to provide critical public services more efficiently and effectively. Researchers accelerate the development of new drugs and treatment protocols. End users benefit from free, personalised consumer experiences such as Internet search, social networking or buying recommendations.

And that is just the beginning. Increasing the control that individuals have over the manner in which their personal data is collected, managed and shared will spur a host of new services and applications. As some put it, personal data will be the new "oil" – a valuable resource of the 21st century. It will emerge as a new asset class touching all aspects of society.

At its core, personal data represents a post-industrial opportunity. It has unprecedented complexity, velocity and global reach. Utilising a ubiquitous communications infrastructure, the personal data opportunity will emerge in a world where nearly everyone and everything are connected in real time. That will require a highly reliable, secure and available infrastructure at its core and robust innovation at the edge. Stakeholders will need to embrace the uncertainty, ambiguity and risk of an emerging ecosystem. In many ways, this opportunity will resemble a living entity and will require new ways of adapting and responding. Most importantly, it will demand a new way of thinking about individuals.

Indeed, rethinking the central importance of the individual is fundamental to the transformational nature of this opportunity because that will spur solutions and insights.

As personal data increasingly becomes a critical source of innovation and value, business boundaries are being redrawn. Profit pools, too, are shifting towards companies that automate and mine the vast amounts of data we continue to generate.[2] Far from certain, however, is how much value will ultimately be created, and who will gain from it. The underlying regulatory, business and technological issues are highly complex, interdependent and ever changing.

But further advances are at risk. The rapid rate of technological change and commercialisation in using personal data is undermining end user confidence and trust. Tensions are rising. Concerns about the misuse of personal data continue to grow. Also mounting is a general public unease about what "they" know about us.[3] Fundamental questions about privacy, property, global governance, human rights – essentially around who should benefit from the products and services built upon personal data – are major uncertainties shaping the opportunity. Yet, we can't just hit the "pause button" and let these issues sort themselves out. Building the legal, cultural, technological and economic infrastructure to enable the development of a balanced personal data ecosystem is vitally important to improving the state of the world.

It is in this context that the **World Economic Forum** launched a project entitled "Rethinking Personal Data" in 2010. The intent of this multiyear project is to bring together a diverse set of stakeholders – private companies, public sector representatives, end user privacy and rights groups, academics and topic experts. The aim is to deepen the collective understanding of how a principled, collaborative and balanced personal data ecosystem can evolve. In particular, this initiative aims to:

- Establish a user-centric framework for identifying the opportunities, risks and collaborative responses in the use of personal data;
- Foster a rich and collaborative exchange of knowledge in the development of cases and pilot studies;
- Develop a guiding set of global principles to help in the evolution of a balanced personal data ecosystem.

EXECUTIVE SUMMARY

Personal Data: Untapped Opportunities For Socioeconomic Growth

The rate of increase in the amount of data generated by today's digital society is astounding. According to one estimate, by 2020 the global volume of digital data will increase more than 40-fold.[4] Beyond its sheer volume, data is becoming a new type of raw material that's on par with capital and labour.[5] As this data revolution era begins, the impact on all aspects of society – business, science, government and entertainment – will be profound.

From a private sector perspective, some of the largest Internet companies such as Google, Facebook and Twitter clearly show the importance of collecting, aggregating, analysing and monetising personal data. These rapidly growing enterprises are built on the economics of personal data.

Governments and public sector institutions are also transforming themselves to use data as a public utility. Many governments have successfully launched e-governance initiatives to improve the efficiency and effectiveness of communication among various public organisations – and with citizens.

But some of the most profound insights are coming from understanding how individuals themselves are creating, sharing and using personal data. On an average day, users globally send around 47 billion (non-spam) emails[6] and submit 95 million "tweets" on Twitter. Each month, users share about 30 billion pieces of content on Facebook.[7] The impact of this "empowered individual" is just beginning to be felt.

However, the potential of personal data goes well beyond these promising beginnings to vast untapped wealth creation opportunities. But unlocking this value depends on several contingencies. The underlying regulatory, business and technological issues are highly complex, interdependent and ever changing.

THE PERSONAL DATA ECOSYSTEM – WHERE WE STAND TODAY

The current personal data ecosystem is fragmented and inefficient. For many participants, the risks and liabilities exceed the economic returns. Personal privacy concerns are inadequately addressed. Regulators, advocates and corporations all grapple with complex and outdated regulations.

Current technologies and laws fall short of providing the legal and technical infrastructure needed to support a well-functioning digital economy. Instead, they represent a patchwork of solutions for collecting and using personal data in support of different institutional aims, and subject to different jurisdictional rules and regulatory contexts (e.g., personal data systems related to banking have different purposes and applicable laws than those developed for the telecom and healthcare sectors).

Consider some of the needs and interests of stakeholders:

Private sector

Private enterprises use personal data to create new efficiencies, stimulate demand, build relationships and generate revenue and profit from their services. But in this drive to develop the "attention economy", enterprises run the risk of violating customer trust. Overstepping the boundary of what users consider fair use can unleash a huge backlash with significant brand implications.

Public sector

Governments and regulators play a vital role in influencing the size and shape of the personal data ecosystem as well as the value created by it. On the one hand, regulators have the mandate to protect the data security and privacy rights of citizens. Therefore, they seek to protect consumers from the potential misuse of their identity. On the other hand, regulators balance this mandate with the need to foster economic growth and promote public well-being. Policy makers around the world are engaged in discussions to enhance legal and regulatory frameworks that will increase disclosure rules, maximise end user control over personal data and penalise non-appropriate usage. Finally, government agencies are using personal data to deliver an array of services for health, education, welfare and law enforcement. The public sector is therefore not just an active player in the personal data universe, but also a stimulator and shaper of the ecosystem – and potentially, the creator of tremendous value for individuals, busi- nesses and economies.

Individuals

Behaviours and attitudes towards personal data are highly fragmented. Demographically, individuals differ in their need for transparency, control and the ability to extract value from the various types of personal data (see Figure 1). According to the research firm International Data Corporation (IDC), individuals' direct or indirect actions generated about 70 per cent of the digital data created in 2010. Activities such as sending an email, taking a digital picture, turning on a mobile phone or posting content online made up this huge volume of data. Younger individuals are more comfortable sharing their data with third parties and social networks – though it remains to be seen whether their behaviours will remain the same or become more risk averse as they age. Older consumers appear to be more sceptical, and demand demonstrably higher security levels from service providers.[8]

Individuals are also becoming more aware of the consequences of not having control over their digital identity and personal data. In 2010 the number of reported incidents of identity theft skyrocketed by 12 per cent.[9]

A Way Forward: The Personal Data Ecosystem

One viable response to this fragmentation is to align key stakeholders (people, private firms and the public sector) in support of one another. Indeed, "win-win-win" outcomes will come from creating mutually supportive incentives, reducing collective inefficiencies and innovating in such a way that collective risks are reduced.

Figure 1: Individual End Users Are At
The Center Of Diverse Types Of Personal Data

Source: Davis, Marc, Ron Martinez and Chris Kalaboukis. "Rethinking
Personal Information – Workshop Pre-read." Invention Arts and World
Economic Forum, June 2010.

This vision includes a future where:
- Individuals can have greater control over their personal data,
  digital identity and online privacy, and they would be better
  compensated for providing others with access to their personal
  data;
- Disparate silos of personal data held in corporations and
  government agencies will more easily be exchanged to increase
  utility and trust among people, private firms and the public sector;
- Government's need to maintain stability, security and individual
  rights will be met in a more flexible, holistic and adaptive manner.

In practical terms, a person's data would be equivalent to their
"money." It would reside in an account where it would be controlled,

managed, exchanged and accounted for just like personal banking services operate today. These services would be interoperable so that the data could be exchanged with other institutions and individuals globally. As an essential requirement, the services would operate over a technical and legal infrastructure that is highly trusted. Maintaining confidence in the integrity, confidentiality, transparency and security of the entire system would require high levels of monitoring.

End User-Centricity: A Critical Determinant In Building The Personal Data Ecosystem

A key element for aligning stakeholder interests and realising the vision of the personal data ecosystem is the concept of end user-centricity. This is a holistic approach that recognises that end users are vital and independent stakeholders in the co-creation and value exchange of services and experiences. A construct designed for the information economy, it breaks from the industrial-age model of the "consumer" – where relationships are captured, developed and owned.

Instead, end user-centricity represents a transformational opportunity. It seeks to integrate diverse types of personal data in a way that was never possible before. This can only be done by putting the end user at the centre of four key principles:

- *Transparency:* Individuals expect to know what data is being captured about them, the manner in which such data is captured or inferred, the uses it will be put to and the parties that have access to it;
- *Trust:* Individuals' confidence that the attributes of availability, reliability, integrity and security are embraced in the applications, systems and providers that have access to their

personal data;

- *Control:* The ability of individuals to effectively manage the extent to which their personal data is shared;
- *Value:* Individuals' understanding of the value created by the use of their data and the way in which they are compensated for it.

Complex Business, Policy And Technological Issues Persist And Require Coordinated Leadership From Firms And The Public Sector

A user-centric ecosystem faces challenges almost as big as its promise, however. Firms, policy makers and governments must resolve a series of critical questions.

For private firms, what are the concrete economic incentives to "empower" individuals with greater choice and control over how their data are used? What are the incentives for greater collaboration within and across industry sectors? How can the returns from using personal data begin to outweigh the risks from a technical, legal and brand-trust perspective?

Policy makers are unique in their mandate to collect, manage and store personal data for purposes such as national defence, security and public safety. They face the issue of finding the right balance between competing priorities: How can they ensure the stability and security of government even as they create incentives for economic investment and innovation? How should they define end users' rights and permissions concerning personal data? How can they more effectively clarify the liabilities? How can they scale globally the concepts of accountability and due process?

Five Areas Of Collective Action

The issues surrounding personal data – political, technological and commercial alike – are numerous and complex. The choices stakeholders make today will influence the personal data ecosystem for years to come. Five key imperatives require action:

1.   Innovate around user-centricity and trust. The personal data ecosystem will be built on the trust and control individuals have in sharing their data. From a technological, policy and sociological sense all stakeholders need to embrace this construct. One particular area of focus is the continued testing and promoting of "trust frameworks" that explore innovative approaches for identity assurance at Internet scale.

2.   Define global principles for using and sharing personal data. Given the lack of globally accepted policies governing the use and exchange of personal data, an international community of stakeholders should articulate and advance core principles of a user-centric personal data ecosystem. These pilots should invite real- world input from a diverse group of individuals who can not only articulate the values, needs and desires of end users, but also the complex and contextual nuances involved in revealing one's digital identity.

3.   Strengthen the dialog between regulators and the private sector. Building on a collective sense of fundamental principles for creating a balanced ecosystem, public and private stakeholders should actively collaborate as the ecosystem begins to take shape. Those responsible for building and deploying the tools (the technologists) should more closely align with those making the rules (regulators).[10]   Establishing the processes to enable stakeholders to formulate, adopt and update a standardised set of rules will serve to create a basic

legal infrastructure. Additionally, collaborating with policy makers as they update legislation to address key questions related to identity and personal data will be essential.[11]

4.   Focus on interoperability and open standards. With the appropriate user controls and legal infrastructure in place, innovations in how personal data moves throughout the value chain will be a key driver for societal and economic value creation. Enabling a secure, trusted, reliable and open infrastructure (both legal and technical) will be vital. Participants should identify best practises and engage with standards bodies, advocacy groups, think tanks and various consortia on the user-centric approaches required to scale the value of personal data.

5.   Continually share knowledge. It's a huge challenge for entities to keep up with new research, policies and commercial developments. To stay current, stakeholders should share insights and learnings on their relevant activities, from both successes as well as failures. After all, the ecosystem's promise is about the tremendous value created when individuals share information about who they are and what they know. Clearly, this principle should also apply to practitioners within the development community.[11] In the US, recent developments emerging from the NSTIC, the Federal Trade Commission and the Department of Commerce warrant attention. In the EU, companies should work with the European Commission's efforts to revise the EU privacy directive and to synchronise legislation across its member states.

SECTION 1:

Personal Data Ecosystem: Overview

Personal Data Is An Evolving And Multifaceted Opportunity

In the era of "anywhere, anytime" connectivity, more people connect to the Internet now in more ways than ever before. One recent estimate projects that in the next 10 years, more than 50 billion devices may connect to the Internet, global devices connected to the Internet many wirelessly (see Figure 2).[12] Global traffic on mobile networks is expected to double each year through 2014.[13]

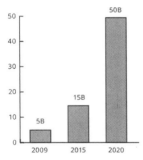

GLOBAL DEVICES CONNECTED
TO THE INTERNET

Sources: Ericsson, Intel

Figure 2: by 2020, more than 50 billion devices will
be connected to the internet

The variety and volume of digital records that can be created, processed and analysed will continue to increase dramatically. By 2020, IDC estimates that the global amount of digital records will increase more than 40-fold (see Figure 3).[14]

As these devices and software continue to come online, they will generate an increasing amount of personal data. The term personal data has several meanings, but we broadly define it as data son or persons.[15]

Think of personal data as the digital record of "everything a person makes and variety of forms that such data assumes constantly, but an initial list of categories includes:

• Digital identity (for example, names, email addresses, phone numbers, physical addresses, demographic information, social network profile information and the like);

GLOBAL DIGITAL DATA
(IN EXABYTES)

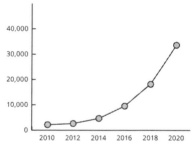

Figure 3: by 2020, digital records will be 44 times larger than in 2009

• Health data (medical history, medical device logs, prescriptions and health insurance coverage);
• Institutional data (governmental, academic and employer data).
• Relationships to other people and organisations (online profiles and contact lists);

- Real-world and online context, activity, interests and behaviour (records of location, time, clicks, searches, browser histories and calendar data);
- Communications data and logs (emails, SMS, phone calls, IM and social network posts);
- Media produced, consumed and shared (in-text, audio, photo, video and other forms of media);
- Financial data (transactions, accounts, credit scores, physical assets and virtual goods); recording activities of users (in contrast to data they volunteer). Examples include Internet browsing preferences, location data when using cell phones or telephone usage behaviour;

Further, organisations can capture these different personal data in a variety of ways:[17]

- Data can be "volunteered" by individuals when they explicitly share information about themselves through electronic media, for example, when someone creates a social network profile or enters credit card information for online purchases;
- "Observed" data is captured by recording activities of users (in contrast to data they volunteer). Examples include Internet browsing preferences, location data when using cell phones.
- Organisations can also discern "inferred" data from individuals, based on the analysis of personal data. For instance, credit scores can be calculated based on a number of factors relevant to an individual's financial history.

Each type of personal data (see Figure 4), volunteered, observed or inferred, can be created by multiple sources (devices, software applications), stored and aggregated by various providers (Web retailers, Internet search engines or utility companies) and analysed for a variety of purposes for many different users (end users, businesses, public organisations).

Regulatory environment

Communication standards

PERSON DATA	PERSON DATA CREATION		STORAGE AGGREGATION	ANALYSIS PRODUCTISATION	CONSUMPTION	
	DEVICES	SOFTWARE				
Volunteered Declared interests Preferences ...	Mobile phones/ smart phones	Apps, OS for PCs	Web retailers	Market research data exchange	End users	
	Desktopn PCs, laptops	Apps, OS for mobile phones	Internet tracking companies	Ad exchanges	Government agencies and public organisations	
Observed Browser history Location ...	Communication networks	Apps, for medical devices	Internet search engines	Medical records exchanges		
			Electronic medical records providers			Small enterprises
Inferred Credit score Future consumption ...	Electronic notepads, readers	Apps, for consumer devices/ appliances	Identity providers	Business intelligence systems	Businesses	Medium enterprises
	Smart appliances		Mobile operators, Internet service providers			
	Sensors			Credit bureaus		Large enterprises
	Smart grids	Network management software	Financial institutions	Public administration		
			Utility companies			
	...	...	...	...		

Figure 4: the personal data ecosystem: a complex web
from data creation to data consumption. Source : Bain & Company

These stakeholders range from the individual end users, who are the sources and subjects of personal data, to the various entities with which they interact. The latter encompass businesses and corporations in different industries to public sector entities like government bodies, NGOs and academia. Personal data flows through this ecosystem, within the boundaries of regulation, to result ultimately in exchanges of monetary and other value.

Points of tension and uncertainty

While tremendous value resides in the data generated by different sources, it often remains untapped. Unlocking the full potential of data will require addressing current uncertainties and points of tension:

- Privacy: Individual needs for privacy vary. Policy makers face a complex challenge while developing legislation and regulations;
- Global governance: There is a lack of global legal interoperability, with each country evolving its own legal and regulatory frameworks;
- Personal data ownership: The concept of property rights is not easily extended to data, creating challenges in establishing usage rights;
- Transparency: Too much transparency too soon presents as much a risk to destabilising the personal data ecosystem as too little transparency;
- Value distribution: Even before value can be shared more equitably, much more clarity will be required on what truly constitutes value for each stakeholder.

Privacy

Privacy continues to be a highly publicised, complex and sensitive issue with multiple perspectives. The complexity surrounding how privacy is conceived and defined creates challenges for policy makers as they seek to address a myriad of issues related to context, culture and personal preference.[18] Adding to the complexity is the pace of technological change and a general lack of guidance on how to accomodate and support various perspectives on "privacy" robustly, flexibly and at global scale (for multiple jurisdictions, cultures and commercial and social settings).[19] Given that many governments are drafting laws and regulations to address privacy concerns, the ambiguity and uncertainty on multiple dimensions heighten the risks that could stall investment and innovation.

Global Governance

Not only are policies and legislation in flux within national borders, there is wide variation across different countries and regions. Indeed, there is no global consensus on two major questions: Which issues related to personal data should be covered by legal and regulatory frameworks? And how should those issues be addressed? While some cross-national agreements exist, for example, the Safe Harbor agreement between the US and the EU,[20] the development of a globally acceptable view of the personal data ecosystem may be years away. This fragmentation stands in the way of fully realising the global impact of the personal data opportunity.

The complexity surrounding how privacy is conceived and defined creates challenges for policy makers as they seek to address a myriad of issues related to context, culture and personal preference.[18] Adding to the complexity is the pace of technological change.

Personal data ownership

"Who owns the data" and "What rights does ownership imply" are two of the most complex issues related to personal data. At first blush, these questions seem simple. Most people would intuitively assert that they own data about themselves and that therefore, they should control who can access, use, aggregate, edit and share it. However, even a cursory look at the issue quickly reveals that the answers are much less clear. Individuals do not "own" their criminal records or credit history. Medical providers are required to keep certain records about patients, even as those patients are allowed to access and share that information with others. Do companies such as Google and Amazon, which aggregate search and purchase histories across millions of users, own the proprietary algorithms they've built upon those click streams?

Given the fluid nature of data and the early stages of the personal data ecosystem, many assert that focusing on the issues of rights management, accountability, due process and the formation of "interoperable" legal frameworks is more productive. It is unlikely that there is a one-size-fits-all approach. A more likely scenario is that different classes of information (financial, health, government records, social, etc.) will get varying degrees of protection – as already is the case in the "pre-digital" world. All such solutions will need to balance individuals' rights to privacy with practical concerns about legitimate needs for critical participants (for example, law enforcement and medical personnel) to access key information when necessary. In addition, practical solutions for issues related to data portability, interoperability and easy-to-implement dashboards for consumers to set and monitor access rights will also need to be developed to overcome the growing friction in the current environment

Transparency

Most end users still remain unaware of just how much they are tagged, tracked and followed on the Internet. Few individuals realise how much data they implicitly give away, how that data might be used or even what is known about them. Some businesses believe the solution lies in "fessing up": simply increasing the transparency on how personal data is used. But that approach not only fails to address the privacy and trust concerns end users have; for many organisations, it often poses a risk to their business model. When customers suddenly find out how their trusted brand of product or service was gathering and using their personal data, they tend to react with outrage, rather than reward the business for its transparency. Similarly, citizens fear Big Brother control and manipulation in the way government uses their personal information. As long as the risk of transparency outweighs the rewards, the personal data ecosystem will remain vulnerable to periodic seismic shocks.

Value distribution

The notion that individuals are producers, creators and owners of their digital activities raises the question: How can value be equitably exchanged? The answer depends on variables like the structure of personal data markets; the amount of public education required; globally governed regulations needed to ensure fair compensation; and the legal frameworks that would ensure accountability and due process.

Uncertainty and tension also exist around the evolution of personal data exchanges and the degree of political empowerment they could create. Some governments can perceive empowered citizens as a disruptive threat to their agenda. Understanding the concept of user-centricity in the context of differing social, cultural and political norms is clearly needed.

Incumbents and disrupters

During the last few decades, a regulatory patchwork has arisen that does not adequately reflect the needs of a competitive global market or the pace of technology. The personal data ecosystem consists of established and new participants; often the regulatory framework covers established business models, but regulation takes time to catch up with emerging, disruptive models. From a regulatory perspective, this can create a fundamentally uneven competitive playing field for creating new personal data services. Companies with established business models – those with large customer bases, legacy investments and trusted brands – typically possess vast amounts of customer data but are legally constrained on its use for commercial purposes. Given those legal constraints, established players are generally conservative in their approach to the market and deeply concerned about unclear liabilities and legal inconsistencies.

On the other hand, many new services and applications are more innovative in their approach and typically use personal data as a central component in their business models. By definition, they tend to fall outside the purview of legacy legal restrictions and typically innovate at the edges of what can be legally done with personal data. A growing concern is the widening chasm between the regulatory oversight on established business models versus new business ideas. Additionally, there are concerns on how current legal and regulatory stakeholders can systemically adapt to the velocity of innovation, the complexity of the ecosystem and the scale of personal impact. Given that a single operational or technical change to a networked communications service can immediately impact hundreds of millions of individuals (if not billions), the capability of policy makers and regulators to understand a given risk and adapt in real time is uncertain. Over time, perceptions of over-regulation and inequity on who can use certain forms of personal data for commercial purposes may create an imbalance among private sector actors.

The risks of an imbalanced ecosystem

The key to unlocking the full potential of data lies in creating equilibrium among the various stakeholders influencing the personal data ecosystem. A lack of balance between stakeholder interests – business, government and individuals – can destabilise the personal data ecosystem in a way that erodes rather than creates value. What follows are just a few possible outcomes that could emerge if any one set of stakeholders gained too strong a role in the ecosystem.

The risk of private sector imbalance

As personal data becomes a primary currency of the digital economy, its use as a means to create competitive advantage will increase. If little regard is paid to the needs of other stakeholders, businesses search- ing for innovative ways to collect, aggregate and use data could end up engaging in a "race to the bottom", building out ever more sophisticated "tricks and traps" to capture personal data.[21] This unfettered mining of personal data would alienate end users and possibly create a backlash.[22]

The risk of public sector imbalance

As countries revise their legal frameworks, policies and regulations to catch up with the unprecedented surge in data, they could inadvertently stifle value creation by over- regulating. Additionally, individual countries may seek to act unilaterally to protect their own citizens from potential harm. The resulting lack of clarity and consistency in policy across countries could slow down innovation and investment.

The risk of end user imbalance

In the absence of engagement with both governments and business, end users could self-organise and create non-commercial alternatives for how their personal data is used. While small groups of dedicated individuals could collaborate on non-commercial products that have the same impact as Wikipedia and Linux, the issues of limited funding, security and lack of governance would remain. Over time, the challenges of managing personal data at a global scale could become overwhelming.

Aligning the different interests to create a true "win-win-win" state for all stakeholders represents a challenge – but it can be done. The solution lies in developing policies, incentives and rewards that motivate all stakeholders – private firms, policy makers, end users – to participate in the creation, protection, sharing and value generation from personal data. The private and public sectors can bring their interests closer by creating an infrastructure that enables the secure and efficient sharing of data across organisations and technologies. End users can be gathered into the fold of the private-public partnership by developing mechanisms that safeguard personal data, validate their content and integrity, and protect ownership. When end users begin to get a share of the value created from their personal data, they will gain more confidence in sharing it.

For such a virtuous cycle to evolve, stakeholders in the personal data ecosystem will need to define new roles and opportunities for the private and public sectors. Greater mutual trust can lead to increased information flows, value creation, and reduced litigation and regulatory costs.

Over time, all stakeholders should hopefully recognise that the collective metric of success is the overall growth of the ecosystem rather than the success of one specific participant. A defining characteristic of such a balanced ecosystem would be end user choice. With the ability to switch easily between vendors, competitive pres- sures would strengthen the control of the end users and help them differentiate between different trust frameworks and service providers.

FUTURE POTENTIAL: SCENARIOS OF A BALANCED PERSONAL DATA ECOSYSTEM

What would the personal data ecosystem offer if the needs of government, private industry and individuals were appropriately balanced?

What follows are some possibilities for the year 2018.

Dianne is a mother of two teenage daughters and a remote caregiver for her father. She's not terribly sophisticated with technology but she uses some social networks to keep up with her friends and family. But as the hub of family care, Dianne is tied to several services that keep her family safe, healthy and informed.

Putting a new spring in her step

Dianne recently upgraded her exercise footwear to a wirelessly networked sports shoe, a product that transforms all of her daily walking into valuable data points. Her health insurance provider encourages exercise through a certified, earned credit system. With minimal data breach risk, walking translates directly into discounts on medications, food and other expenses for not only herself but also her father and daughters linked to her health savings account. This lets Dianne take better care of her loved ones, which is a more powerful motivator than her own health and wellness. The initial savings helped convert her children to regular walking as well. What was routine is now a game as the family competes in active walking challenges with one another, all the while providing better healthcare for everyone.

Transparency – data usage disclosure
Control – opt-in participation with immediate feedback in rewards balance
Trust – certified by identity consortium across health, finance and other service providers
Value – discounts powered by data collection that can be applied to many different needs

Source: frog design research, 2010

At ease and secure

Dianne's old anxiety over identity theft has been less of a worry since the Personal Data Protection and Portability Act went into effect, legislation the government passed in 2014 granting citizens greater control and transparency over their digital information. Her employer provides a private, certified Data-Plus Integrity Plan that monitors and ensures the personal data of her whole family and is portable across jobs. Dianne feels more at ease about her daughters' social habits online with the Parent Teachers Association-endorsed TeenSecure. A comprehensive activity summary and alert system means Dianne no longer feels like a spy, monitoring her kids and investigating every new social site. Her daughters' access is managed, tracked and protected by a trusted socially acceptable source. Dianne receives simple, convenient monthly statements that highlight both the activity and stored value of her data. As an added benefit, various retailers offer coupons and discounts during the holidays, in exchange for Dianne allowing them to use some of this activity data as a second currency.

Transparency – single view of all activity Control – monitoring of dependents
Trust – government and consumer advocacy backed
Value – peace of mind and stored value

When Dianne's father moved into managed care with early-stage symptoms of Alzheimer's disease, her insurance carrier provided her with control of her father's medications and recommended an online dashboard-like tool adapted to his condition. The service is offered in a partnership with the Alzheimer's Research Foundation, as well as the Department of Public Health, which have connected her father's information and medical health records to her Data-Plus Integrity Plan. This provides Dianne with on-demand monitoring services, medication compliance tracking and feedback on how he is feeling. She is also able to keep tabs on his finances. Dianne hopes that through the sharing of her father's medical condition, they may one day find a cure. In the meantime, her in-person visits are less about evaluating his condition and much more about spending time together.

Transparency – permission of data access
Control – progression of need increases access
Trust – family-centric data safeguards
Value – transferable control

Source: frog design research, 2010

Key enablers of a balanced ecosystem

While building a balanced ecosystem around personal data will require significant commitment from all stakeholders, four critical enablers are apparent:

- An easy-to-understand user-centric approach to the design of systems, tools and policies, with an emphasis on transparency, trust, control and value distribution;
- Mechanisms for enhancing trust among all parties in digital transactions;
- Greater interoperability among existing data silos;
- An expanded role for government, such that governments can use their purchasing power to help shape commercially available products and solutions that the private sector can then leverage.

User-centricity

The concept of user-centricity is the central pivot point of the personal data ecosystem. With greater control placed in the hands of individuals, new efficiencies and capabilities can emerge. Many perceive this shift in power as highly disruptive. It creates a diversity of perspectives on if, how and when the "pivot for the people" might occur. In short, the transition to user-centricity is anything but simple. It's hard collectively to frame and act upon it due to the significant differences in cultural, geopolitical and institutional norms.

Globally, there is a growing consensus that there is an urgent need for greater trust associated with online identities. People find the increasing complexity of managing multiple user names and passwords across different organisations a major inconvenience. Additionally, as online fraud and identity theft continue to skyrocket, people demand greater assurances about who they are interacting with. As secure and trusted online relationships are established with individuals and various institutions, silos of information that were previously unavailable can also become easier to incorporate into personalised solutions.

A market is now taking shape to address these concerns on personal identity. In fact, an ecosystem of interoperable identity service providers offering solutions that are secure, easy to use and market based is in its early stages of development.[23] As more services move online (in particular, health and financial services), the infrastructure costs of ensuring the identity of who can use a given online offering will continue to escalate. The value of paying a third party for trusted digital identities will most likely continue to increase as these services reduce both the cost of fraud as well as the risk of offering additional value-added services[24] (see sidebar, "End user principles").

Trust enablers

Interviews and discussions with leading privacy advocates, regulatory experts and business leaders lead to an overwhelming consensus: trust is another key ingredient required for creating value from today's oceans of disparate personal data. Without the establishment of trust, particularly the trust of the end user, a personal data ecosystem that benefits all stakeholders will never coalesce.

END USER PRINCIPLES

Transparency	Trust
What is a meaningful way to understand transparency, and who provides the lens to the user? People naturally expect the right to see, and thus know, the data that is being captured about them. If that right is not respected, they feel deceived and exploited. Upon seeing this reflection of themselves through their personal data, people start to feel a sense of personal connection and ownership, leading to the desire for control. How-ever, people struggle to form a mental model of something that is fragmented and abstract in nature. This creates a challenge: what is invisible must be revealed, made tangible and ultimately be connected across different points of access.	Which investments in building trust will help users feel comfortable allowing others to access their data? Personal data is difficult, if not impossi- ble, to un-share. Once shared, it gains a life of its own. Given the risk of unintended consequences, people rely heav- ily on trust to guide their decisions. But how is trust formed? Different thresh- olds of trust exist for different types of data. While a majority of people accept a certain level of risk, viewing it as an opportunity cost for gaining something, the benefits are often coupled with feel- ings of anxiety and fear. Such concerns will continue to limit the potential value of personal data until a comprehensible model for creating and certifying trust relationships is adopted on a large scale.

Control	Value
What are the primary parameters that influence how users will want to control their data, and how are they adapted to different contexts?	What measures must be taken to ensure that data created today is a mutually beneficial asset in the future?
People naturally want control over data that is both about them and often created by them. Control can be exercised in three ways:	The value of personal data is wildly subjective. Many business models have emerged that encourage and capitalise on the flow of that data. Consumers are becoming increasingly aware of the value of the data they generate even in mun- dane interactions like a Google search.
(a) directly through explicit choices; (b) indirectly by defining rules; (c) by proxy.	While direct personal data has an inherent value, secondary inferred data can often be mined and interpreted to produce new information of equal or greater value. The long-term impact of the aggregation and unchecked dissemination of this information is unknown. Digital behaviour today may yield positive distributed value across the ecosystem in the near term, but can have detrimental consequences for the end user in the future.
People's perception of a given situation will determine whether they choose to exercise control. The more subtle qualities of an experience (such as feedback, convenience and understanding) will determine how they choose to exercise that control.	

To use a metaphor, trust is the lubricant that enables a virtuous cycle for the ecosystem: it engenders stakeholder participation, which, in turn, drives the value creation process. For such a virtuous cycle to evolve, mutual trust needs to be at the foundation of all relationships. Increased trust leads to increased information flows, sharing and value creation and reduces litigation and regulatory costs.

Increasing interoperability and the sharing of personal data

Promoting solutions that drive the exchange and "movement" of personal data in a secure, trusted and authenticated manner is also essential. Today, it is difficult to share personal data across private and public organisations and jurisdictions. This is due to a combination of technological, regulatory and business factors. Decades-old privacy laws and policies could not have fore seen the emergence of digital personal data as a valuable asset. Inadequate legislation has thus made standards surrounding the use of personal data inconsistent.

Furthermore, many organisations employ legacy technology systems and databases that were created in proprietary, closed environments. As a result, personal data today is often isolated in silos – bound by organisational, data type, regional or service borders – each focusing on a limited set of data types and services.

To achieve global scale, technical, semantic and legal infrastructures will need to be established that are both resilient and interoperable. The US National Strategy for Trusted Identities in Cyberspace notes three types of interoperability for identity solutions:[25]

- Technical interoperability – The ability for different technologies to communicate and exchange data based upon well-defined and widely adopted interface standards;
- Semantic interoperability – The ability of each end point to communicate data and have the receiving party understand the message in the sense intended by the sending party;
- Legal interoperability – Common business policies and processes (e.g., identity proofing and vetting) related to the transmission,

receipt and accept-standards, existing pilots and collaboration with industry and advocacy groups, a functional degree of interoperability can be achieved in a shorter time frame.

It is important to stress that the call for interoperability does not equate to working exclusively with standards bodies. In many cases standards take too long. By leveraging open protocols, de facto standards, existing pilots and collaboration with industry and advocacy groups, a functional degree of interoperability can be achieved in a shorter time frame.

Despite this "need for speed", the levels of reliability, integrity and security for both the individual and the computing infrastructure cannot be understated. The broad private sector support to cooperate in the sharing of personal data will bring with it extremely high technical, legal and performance requirements.

Government as enabler

Governments have a vital role to play in accelerating the growth of a balanced personal data ecosystem. Their influence manifests itself along three primary dimensions.

First, they play a dominant role in crafting the legal and regulatory environments that shape what is possible in the ecosystem. This is a challenging role in many respects. Within the national context, regulators are being asked to balance consumer protection with the need to create a business environment conducive to innovation, growth and job creation. On top of that, many global industry participants are turning to national and regional regulatory bodies to harmonise guidelines to facilitate global platforms.

Second, governments are active participants in ongoing experiments regarding how the personal data ecosystem can be harnessed to achieve important social goals such as providing more efficient and cost-effective services to citizens, stopping epidemics before they become pandemics and using data- mining techniques to enhance national security.

Third, and perhaps most importantly, given their purery, governments can write specifications for everything from security protocols to end user interfaces and data portability options. Successful projects can serve as proof points and major references for innovative solutions.

Hands-on experience gained in leveraging personal data for government services and objectives, combined with insights gleaned from negotiations with vendors, can give regulatory deliberations a very practical bent, which should be beneficial chasing power, governments are in a position to influence significantly commercially available solutions. In crafting requests for proposals to help modernise service delivery, governments can write specifications for everything from security protocols to end user interfaces and data portability options. Successful projects can serve as proof points and major references for innovative solutions.

Hands-on experience gained in leveraging personal data for government services and objectives, combined with insights gleaned from negotiations with vendors, can give regulatory deliberations a very practical bent, which should be beneficial to all parties.

SECTION 2: STAKEHOLDER TRUST AND TRUST FRAMEWORKS

Achieving a high level of stakeholder trust requires a set of legal and technical structures to govern the interactions of participants within the ecosystem. The concept of trust frameworks is emerging as an increasingly attractive means for the personal data ecosystem to scale in a balanced manner. Trust frameworks consist of documented specifications selected by a particular group (a "trust community"). These govern the laws, contracts and policies undergirding the technologies selected to build the identity system. The specifications ensure the system reliability that is crucial for creating trust within the ecosystem.

The Trust Framework Model

The Open Identity Trust Framework model (OITF) is a working example. Built to Internet scale, it offers a single sign-on environment for trust between relying parties and end users. The model addresses two problems with the way end users and relying parties interact with the Internet today:

- The proliferation of user names and passwords;
- The inability of relying parties to verify the identity of other entities.

Most people can relate to the first problem. Almost every website requires visitors to establish a user name and password, and invariably requires the sharing of such personal data as name, address and credit card information. Not only is this inconvenient, it's unsafe. It puts our personal data onto every server with which we interact, increasing the odds that our data may be compromised.

The second problem trust frameworks address is the lack of certainty about online identities. In most of today's Internet transactions, neither the user nor the relying party is completely sure of the other's identity. That creates a huge opening for identity theft and fraud. In 2009, more than $3 billion in online revenue was lost due to fraud in North America.[27] Some $550 million of that was money lost by individual US consumers.[28] The hope is that with a richer, scalable and more flexible identity management system, these losses can be reduced.

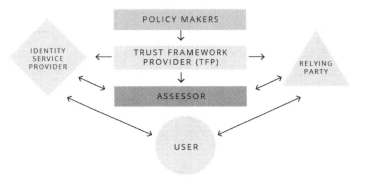

Figure 5: The open identity trust framework model (Source: OITF)

The model defines the following roles (see Figure 5) to support Internet-scale identity management:

- Policy makers decide the technical, operational and legal requirements for exchanges of identity information among the group they govern;
- Trust framework providers translate these requirements into the building blocks of a trust framework. They then certify identity verification providers that provide identity management services

in accordance with the specifications of the trust framework. Finally, the trust framework provider recruits assessors responsible for auditing and ensuring that framework participants adhere to the specifications;

- Identity providers (IdPs) issue, verify and maintain online credentials for an individual user. Relying parties accept these credentials and have firm assurances that the IdP has analysed and validated the individual user;

- Assessors evaluate IdPs and relying parties, and certify that they are capable of following the trust framework provider's blueprint.

Within such a trust framework model, end users can access multiple sites (relying parties) using a single credential issued by an identity provider. On their part, the sites can rest assured about the identities of the individuals they are doing business with. This screening is similar to how a car rental agent trusts that a driver can legally operate an automobile because he or she has a valid driver's licence.

With such a framework, users would need only to share less sensitive personal data with relying parties. No longer would they have to enter their name, address and credit card information in order to purchase a Web service. Using the trust framework, they would share the minimum amount of data to complete the transaction. In some cases, that may simply amount to verification of the availability of the funds being transmitted to the relying party.

Personal data services

The trust framework model will bring benefits to end users in the form of increased privacy and a more seamless and convenient Web experience. But such advantages can be extended through the related concepts of personal data services and vendor relationship management (VRM).

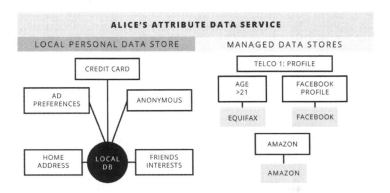

Figure 6: Personal data services store end users' data and provide applications that enable them to manage, share and gain benefit from their personal data[29]

Source: The Eclipse Foundation

Personal data services provide the safe means by which an end user can store, manage, share and gain benefit from his or her personal data. These data can range from such self-asserted attributes as the individual's likes, preferences and interests to such managed and verified attributes as a person's age, credit score or affiliations, and histories with external entities like firms, government agencies and the like (see Figure 6).

Personal data services consolidate end users' digital identity, allowing them to control which third parties are entitled to access – along with how, when and at what price. VRM extends this control to the realm of realising direct value – monetary or in kind – from the personal data stored and managed by personal data services providers.

These emerging concepts will help build stakeholder trust and herald additional benefits for end users and relying parties alike. Indeed, some promising trials are already under way. Yet more testing will be needed to resolve some open questions about the viability of these concepts.

Key uncertainties of trust frameworks

Trust frameworks and personal data services are concepts in their infancy. Despite encouraging pilots in the US and the UK, they need further refinement and testing to fulfil their promise. Implementations thus far have primarily been at websites where the level of assurance required is relatively low, such as those enabling blogging or providing news content. They need to be deployed in environments that encompass more highrisk transactions, such as logging into a bank account. Only then will proponents know if these ideas can achieve Internet scale.

Risks and uncertainties also surround the business models for both identity providers and relying parties. While a large number of private enterprises have begun working in this space (Acxiom, AOL, Citibank, Equifax, Google and PayPal) the economics are unclear.[30]

From the perspective of relying parties, the benefits of transitioning to a user-centric model are still emerging. In this new approach, relying parties will be constrained on collecting data for free and will need to start paying for end user data. While some believe that an aggregated and holistic view of an individual would be more valuable, the balance of trade between what relying parties would be willing to share versus the new insights and efficiencies they would gain from a holistic user-centric view are unclear.

However, the cost of online fraud and risk mitigation could be enough to make relying parties seriously consider participating in a more collaborative model. On average, on- line fraud represented 1.2 per cent of a Web retailer's revenue in 2009.[31]

Finally, building end user awareness is another uncertainty. How can firms communicate to individuals the advantages of managing their personal data? For a start, companies must themselves fully understand the convenience, value proposition, contextual nuances and usability of personal data dashboards. Further investigation is therefore needed into applications and services that provide end users with convenient, contextually relevant and simplified control over their data.

SECTION 3: CONCLUSIONS

Personal data will continue to increase dramatically in both quantity and diversity, and has the potential to unlock significant economic and societal value for end users, private firms and public organisations alike.

The business, technology and policy trends shaping the nascent personal ecosystem are complex, interrelated and constantly changing. Yet a future ecosystem that both maximises economic and societal value – and spreads its wealth across all stakeholders – is not only desirable but distinctly possible. To achieve that promise, industries and public bodies must take coordinated actions today. Leaders should consider taking steps in the following five areas:

1. INNOVATE AROUND USER-CENTRICITY AND TRUST

Where we stand today

Innovative concepts already exist on how personal data can be shared in a way that allows all stakeholders to trust the integrity and safety of this data. Examples of such trust frameworks include the Open Identity Trust Framework and Kantara's Identity Assurance Framework. However, no truly large-scale application of a trust framework has yet been rolled out. As a consequence, we remain uncertain about how to take advantage of personal data while still aligning stakeholder interests. Also unanswered are questions such as: What are the incentives for stakeholders to participate in trust frameworks? What are the business model mechanics? Who will pay for identity provider services?

What is required and why

Complex blueprints for Internet business models typically come to life in iterative steps. For example, the retail banking sector evolved online through successive phases of change. Trust frameworks need similar pressure testing in large- scale applications to prove these concepts can be instrumental in unlocking economic and societal value. Addition- ally, end user participation in testing and developing these trust frameworks is crucial. Offering more transparency on how personal data is used and educating end users on the benefits they can extract from such applications – two areas lacking in the ecosystem today – will significantly strengthen trust among all stakeholders.

Recommended next steps

Private firms and policy makers should consider the following next steps:

- Invest in open and collaborative trials orchestrated by end user privacy groups or academics;
- Integrate principles surrounding end user trust and data protection into the development of new services and platforms (the concept of "privacy by design"), particularly when designing new "e-government" platforms;
- Engage with leading innovators and end user advocacy groups to explore the further applications for, and development of internationally accepted, user-centric principles. Additionally, a set of commonly accepted terms of, trust frameworks.

2. DEFINE GLOBAL PRINCIPLES FOR USING AND SHARING PERSONAL DATA

Where we stand today

Privacy-related laws and police enforcement differ significantly across jurisdictions, often based on cultural, political and historical contexts. Attempts to align such policies have largely failed.[32] But the need is growing. Many Internet services, in particular those based upon cloud computing delivery models, require the cross-jurisdictional exchange of personal data to function at optimal levels.

What is required and why

The downside of the current divergence in regulatory frameworks manifests itself in several ways. First, companies striving to provide products and services based upon personal data see significant complexity costs associated with compliance. As a result of these costs, they may choose not to offer their product and services in certain smaller markets, where the cost of doing business may outweigh incremental profits. That decision to opt out obviously hurts the users who cannot access the services. Less obvious is the fact that users with access are also hurt, as the value of many of these services increases with the number of users.

A truly global and seamless exchange of personal data will not emerge without a set of internationally accepted, user-centric principles. Additionally, a set of commonly accepted terms and definitions – a taxonomy – surrounding personal data concepts must be created to allow unencumbered dialog.   Although it is unrealistic to hope to develop globally accepted standards and frameworks   while national and regional versions are still in significant flux, establishing a standing, cross-regional dialog will allow for more rapid harmonisation once regulatory environments do begin to stabilise.

It is imperative for private sector firms to participate in at least some of these dialogs, as they can share real-world perspectives on the cost and challenges of dealing with divergent regulations and can help public sector officials adapt pragmatic and consistent policies.

Recommended next steps

- Policy makers and private firms should launch an international dialog to stay informed about proposed laws and policies that would have a global bearing on their markets. This dialog should encompass governments, international bodies such as the World Trade Organization, end user privacy rights groups and representation from the private sector. It should include not only US and European Union members, but interested parties from the Asia-Pacific region and emerging countries;
- Among the outputs of this body would be an agreed-upon benchmark measuring the effectiveness of national regulations and their impact on free markets. This could prove vital in unearthing and spreading best practises that could ultimately guide the development of consistent national policies.

3. STRENGTHEN THE DIALOG BETWEEN REGULATORS AND THE PRIVATE SECTOR

Where we stand today

The roots of today's data privacy laws grew from the aspirational principles of the early 1980s, which reflected a consensus about the need for standards to ensure both individual privacy and information flows.[33] But over the last two decades, these principles have been translated very differently into national policies in the US, the European Union and the Asia-Pacific. Although most of these laws aim to maximise data protection and individual control, many experts question their practical effectiveness given technological advances. Some governments, such as in the US and European Union, are therefore revising their policies.

What is required and why

Topic experts and executives involved in the "Rethinking Personal Data" project agree that self-regulation of markets related to personal data is not a desirable outcome for all stakeholders. Instead, national and regional agencies must adopt 21st-century digital policies that promote and accelerate favourable behaviour from all market participants.

Recommended next steps

- **In the United States:** Private firms should closely watch developments of the National Strategy for Trusted Identities in Cyberspace programme and the privacy bill – and seek ways to contribute to them. Private firms and advocacy groups need to be in constant dialog with the US Department of Commerce, the Federal Trade Commission and other bodies tohelpshapefuturelegislation and policies;
- **In the European Union:** Private firms should collaborate with the European Commission in its move to revise the EU privacy directive and to synchronise legislation across its member states. A revised EU privacy directive is scheduled to go into effect in

2011, after a period of public consultation through the European Commission's website during January;[34]

- **In other countries:** In other regions that differ from the US or the EU in cultural or social norms, very different paths in adopting policy frameworks will be required. However, given the global relevance of many such markets in the future digital economy, private firms and policy makers should not just wait and see. One initial step in making progress could be to seek ways to harmonise fragmented national privacy policies. For example, a starting point in Asia could be the Asia Pacific Privacy Charter Initiative, which, since 2003, aims to align privacy policies and to promote best practises in regulatory and legislative frameworks in the region.

4. Focus on interoperability and open standards

Where we stand today

A large variety of syntax and semantic standards exist to describe and share personal data. Most of those standards are proprietary and were often invented in an ad hoc manner without broader consulta- tion with industry peers. While some open standards are emerging – for example, in the realm of digital identities, standards include ISO/IEEE, Mozilla and OIX – no standards are in place for many other data types, particularly new ones. The history of the Internet shows that open standards can improve data portability significantly. One example from the 1980s was the advent of the simple mail transfer protocol (SMTP), which superseded various proprietary email standards.[35]

What is required and why

If we posit that the highest potential for economic and societal value creation lies in the aggregation of different personal data types, the implication is clear: To enable the seamless sharing of personal data across organisational borders, private firms and the public sector will require common communication standards, system architectures, accepted personal data terms and definitions, and standard interface design specifications.

Recommended next steps

- Private firms, in particular those from the information communication technologies sector, should participate in initiatives that aim to align today's jumble of standards. The Open Web Foundation is one such example: it has helped companies define commonly accepted standards and avoid competitive deadlocks;[36]
- Private firms and public bodies should use the knowledge gained from ongoing pilot tests of trust frameworks and related services to inform standardisation bodies, such as the IEEE;
- To build momentum, firms and public organisations should monitor the ongoing dialog to identify the most valuable types of personal data and focus standardisation efforts on those first.

5. CONTINUALLY SHARE KNOWLEDGE

Where we stand today

Interested sponsors continually hold a large number of conferences, events, websites, private-public discussions and blogs on the different aspects of the personal data ecosystem. Even for active dialog participants, it's challenging to keep up with the latest developments and research. Some platforms are aiming to synthesise this ongoing dialog, yet none has yet reached a critical mass with private and public stakeholders.

What is required and why

The goal is to aggregate the key insights– from both successful and unsuccessful initiatives – in a timely and unbiased manner. This would enable the sharing of lessons learned, right from the introduction of new personal data services to the development of further research activities.

Recommended next steps

* Private firms should nominate a central gatekeeper in the organisation who actively contributes to the personal data dialog. That person's purview would not only include privacy but also encompass a business development and strategic perspective;

* Private and public sector representatives should invest in a jointly run organisation that facilitates a truly global dialog about personal data – one that stretches across industries and regions. Given private companies' increasing propensity to be multinational, the onus is on them to pressure their respective governments to think on a global scale.

GLOSSARY OF TERMS

END USER

This term refers to individual consumers, citizens or persons about and from whom personal data is created. End users are also able to participate in the use and proliferation of personal data via related services, applications and technology. End users are typically represented on a broad, public scale by consumer advocacy groups, such as the American Civil Liberties Union (ACLU) in the United States.

END USER-CENTRICITY

End user-centricity refers to the concept of organising the rules and policies of the personal data ecosystem around the key principles that end users value: transparency into what data is captured, control over how it is shared, trust in how others use it and value attributable because of it.

IDENTITY PROVIDER

Identity providers (IdPs) issue, verify and maintain online credentials for an individual user. Relying parties accept these credentials and have solid assurances that the IdP has analysed and validated the individual user in accordance with specifications.

PERSON[37]

A person can be defined as a natural person, a legal person or a digital persona. A natural person refers to a specific human being with an individual physical body (e.g., John Smith). A legal person refers to a body of persons or an entity (as a corporation) considered as having many of the rights and responsibilities of a natural person and in particular the capacity to sue and be sued (e.g., John Smith and Associates, LLC). Legal persons encompass a wide range of legal entities, including corporations, partnerships, limited liability companies, cooperatives, municipalities, sovereign states, intergovernmental organisations and some international organisations. A digital persona (or identity) can be understood as a digital representation of a set of claims made about a person, either by themselves or by another person (e.g., JohnSmith@gmail.com or JohnSmith@facebook.com). Note that a natural person may have multiple digital personae.

PERSONAL DATA

We broadly define personal data as data and metadata (i.e., data about data) relating to an identified or identifiable person or persons. Our definition is based upon European Union Directive 95/46/ EC. Personal data can be created in multiple ways, including: (1) volunteered data, which is created and explicitly shared by individuals (e.g., social network profiles); (2) observed data, which is captured by recording the actions of individuals (e.g.,location data when using cell phones); and (3) inferred data, which is data about individuals based on analysis of volunteered or observed information (e.g., credit scores).

PRIVACY[38]

The term privacy has two separate meanings. The public use of the term privacy is very broad, and it is used to reference nearly anything that has to do with personal data and more generally the perceived rights of an individual in relationship to a group. The legal meaning is much narrower. In US domestic law, it refers to a constitutional right (as interpreted by the courts) and several specific tort rights. Privacy tort rights, which are based mostly in common law (i.e., cases as opposed to statutes), are generally categorised to include the protection of solitude and has developed to include protection of "personality." Privacy tort "causes of action" are generally recognised to protect against four kinds of wrongs against the invasion of privacy. That includes (1) the appropriation of a person's picture or name by another for their commercial advantage (generally the promotion of goods), (2) the intrusion on a person's affairs or seclusion (if objectionable to a reasonable person), (3) the publication of facts that place a person in a false light (for example, publicly attributing an action or statement to a person that he or she did not make), and (4) public disclosures of private facts about the person. Both the public and legal meanings have one thing in common; they are both associated with "protection from harm" of the affected person.

PRIVATE SECTOR (OR COMPANIES)

Within the context of the personal data ecosystem, the "private sector" refers to for-profit companies and private organisations involved in the capture, storage, analysis and sharing of personal data for the purposes of developing – and monetising – related services and applications. Private sector participants are not limited by size or industry group: they are any private entity that directly manipulates personal data for explicit financial gain.

PUBLIC SECTOR (OR AGENCIES)

Within the context of the personal data ecosystem, the public sector refers to governments (and their agencies) and nonprofit public organisations that are involved in the passing of legislation and policies that regulate the capture and use of personal data within their respective jurisdictions. Public sector entities also participate in capturing and storing personal data (e.g., social security information), as well as the development of related services and applications.

RELYING PARTY

In the context of trust frameworks, relying parties are typically businesses or organisations that rely on personal data as a means to verify the identities of their customers or partners. Without reliable and verifiable information, these transactions can be fraught with risks, including fraud.

TRUST FRAMEWORKS

Within the context of online and digital transactions, a trust framework is a formalised specification of policies and rules to which a participant (e.g., an end user, relying party or identity provider) must conform in order to be trusted. These policies include requirements around identity, security, privacy, data protection, technical profiles and assessor qualifi- cations. This trust may be subject to different levels of assurance or protection, which are explicitly made clear to all parties.[39]

The World Economic Forum is an independent international organisation committed to improving the state of the world by engaging business, political, academic and other leaders of society to shape global, regional and industry agendas. Incorporated as a foundation in 1971, and based in Geneva, Switzerland, the World Economic Forum is impartial and not-for-profit; it is tied to no political, partisan or national interests.

World Economic Forum 91- 93 route de la Capite
CH – 1223 Cologny/Geneva Switzerland
Tel.: +41 (0) 22 869 1212
Fax: +41 (0) 22 786 2744
email: contact@weforum.org www.weforum.org

APPENDIX B

A World That Counts
Mobilising the Data Revolution
for Sustainable Development

This report is the work of the UN Secretary-General's Independent Expert Advisory Group on the Data Revolution for Sustainable Development: Enrico Giovannini (Co-Chair, Italy) Robin Li (Co-Chair, China), TCA Anant (India), Shaida Badiee (Iran), Carmen Barroso (Brazil), Robert Chen (United States), Choi Soon-hong (Republic of Korea), Nicolas de Cordes (Belgium), Fu Haishan (China), Johannes Jütting (Germany), Pali Lehohla (South Africa), Tim O'Reilly (United States), Sandy Pentland (United States), Rakesh Rajani (Tanzania), Juliana Rotich (Kenya), Wayne Smith (Canada), Eduardo Sojo GarzaAldape (Mexico), Gabriella Vukovich (Hungary), Alicia Barcena (ECLAC), Robert Kirkpatrick (Global Pulse), Eva Jespersen (UNDP), Edilberto Loaiza (UNFPA), Katell Le Goulven (UNICEF), Thomas Gass (ex officio) and Amina J. Mohammed (ex officio)

The United Nations Secretary-General's Independent Expert Advisory Group on a Data Revolution for Sustainable Development (IEAG) thanks the hundreds of individuals and organisations that contributed online and during the face-to-face meetings organised in New York and in Geneva, as well as other meetings attended by IEAG members. Contributions, including in-kind, are gratefully acknowledged, including those from UNDP, DfID, UN Global Pulse, ECE, UN Secretariat - including DESA, DGACM, DM, and EOSG - UN Millennium Campaign, UN NGLS, Microsoft and UN Foundation.

We gratefully acknowledge help and advice from many others, especially Muhammad Abdullahi, Youlia Antonova, René Clausen Nielsen, Joe Colombano, Marie-Ange Diegue, Jaspreet Doung, Tala Dowlatshahi, Eleonore Fournier-Tombs, Caya Johnson, Eva Kaplan, Kate Krukiel, Paul Ladd, Yongyi Min, Keiko Osaki-Tomita, Anna Ortubia, Paul Pacheco, Matthias Reister, Stefan Schweinfest, Frances Simpson-Allen, Corinne Woods and Wailan Wu.

Independent Expert Advisory Group Secretary: Claire Melamed

Research team: Luis Gonzalez Morales, Yu-Chieh Hsu, Jennifer Poole, Benjamin Rae, Ian Rutherford.

Produced by: Independent Expert Advisory Group Secretariat
Copyright Independent Expert Advisory Group Secretariat 2014 ©
For more information please visit: www.undatarevolution.org

EXECUTIVE SUMMARY
Mobilising the data revolution for sustainable development

Data are the lifeblood of decision-making and the raw material for accountability. Without high-quality data providing the right information on the right things at the right time; designing, monitoring and evaluating effective policies becomes almost impossible.

New technologies are leading to an exponential increase in the volume and types of data available, creating unprecedented possibilities for informing and transforming society and protecting the environment. Governments, companies, researchers and citizen groups are in a ferment of experimentation, innovation and adaptation to the new world of data, a world in which data are bigger, faster and more detailed than ever before. This is the data revolution.

Some are already living in this new world. But too many people, organisations and governments are excluded because of lack of resources, knowledge, capacity or opportunity. There are huge and growing inequalities in access to data and information and in the ability to use it.

Data needs improving. Despite considerable progress in recent years, whole groups of people are not being counted and important aspects of people's lives and environmental conditions are still not measured. For people, this can lead to the denial of basic rights, and for the planet, to continued environmental degradation. Too often, existing data remain unused because they are released too late or not at all, not well- documented and harmonized, or not available at the level of detail needed for decision-making.

As the world embarks on an ambitious project to meet new Sustainable Development Goals (SDGs), there is an urgent need to mobilise the data revolution for all people and the whole planet in order to monitor progress, hold governments accountable and foster sustainable development. More diverse, integrated, timely and trustworthy information can lead to better decision-making and real-time citizen feedback. This in turn enables individuals, public and private institutions, and companies to make choices that are good for them and for the world they live in.

This report sets out the main opportunities and risks presented by the data revolution for sustainable development. Seizing these opportunities and mitigating these risks requires active choices, especially by governments and international institutions.
Without immediate action, gaps between developed and developing countries, between information-rich and information-poor people, and between the private and public sectors will widen, and risks of harm and abuses of human rights will grow.

An urgent call for action: key recommendations

The strong leadership of the United Nations (UN) is vital for the success of this process. The Independent Expert Advisory Group (IEAG),
established in August 2014, offers the UN Secretary-
General several key recommendations for actions to be taken in the near future, summarised below:

1. **Develop a global consensus on principles and standards:** The disparate worlds of public, private and civil society data and statistics providers need to be urgently brought together to build trust and confidence among data users. We propose that

the UN establish a process whereby key stakeholders create a "Global Consensus on Data", to adopt principles concerning legal, technical, privacy, geospatial and statistical standards which, among other things, will facilitate openness and information exchange and promote and protect human rights.

2. **Share technology and innovations for the common good:** To create mechanisms through which technology and innovation can be shared and used for the common good, we propose to create a global "Network of Data Innovation Networks", to bring together the organisations and experts in the field. This would: contribute to the adoption of best practices for improving the monitoring of SDGs, identify areas where common data-related infrastructures could address capacity problems and improve efficiency, encourage collaborations, identify critical research gaps and create incentives to innovate.

3. **New resources for capacity development:** Improving data is a development agenda in its own right, and can improve the targeting of existing resources and spur new economic opportunities. Existing gaps can only be overcome through new investments and the strengthening of capacities. A new funding stream to support the data revolution for sustainable development should be endorsed at the "Third International Conference on Financing for Development", in Addis Ababa in July 2015. An assessment will be needed of the scale of investments, capacity development and technology transfer that is required, especially for low income countries; and proposals developed for mechanisms to leverage the creativity and resources of the private sector. Funding will also be needed

to implement an education program aimed at improving people's, infomediaries' and public servants' capacity and data literacy to break down barriers between people and data.

4.   **Leadership for coordination and mobilisation:** A UN-led "Global Partnership for Sustainable Development Data" is proposed, to mobilise and coordinate the actions and institutions required to make the data revolution serve sustainable development, promoting several initiatives, such as:

- A "World Forum on Sustainable Development Data" to bring together the whole data ecosystem to share ideas and experiences for data improvements, innovation, advocacy and technology transfer. The first Forum should take place at the end of 2015, once the SDGs are agreed;
- A "Global Users Forum for Data for SDGs", to ensure feedback loops between data producers and users, help the international community to set priorities and assess results;
- Brokering key global public-private partnerships for data sharing.

5.   **Exploit some quick wins on SDG data:** Establishing a "SDGs data lab" to support the development of a first wave of SDG indicators, developing an SDG analysis and visualisation platform using the most advanced tools and features for exploring data, and building a dashboard from diverse data sources on "the state of the world".

Never again should it be possible to say "we didn't know". No one should be invisible. This is the world we want – a world that counts.

for more information on the composition, terms of reference and work of the leag, see www.undatarevolution.org

1   WHAT IS THE DATA REVOLUTION
    FOR SUSTAINABLE DEVELOPMENT?

Data are the lifeblood of decision-making. Without data, we cannot know how many people are born and at what age they die; how many men, women and children still live in poverty; how many children need educating; how many doctors to train or schools to build; how public money is being spent and to what effect; whether greenhouse gas emissions are increasing or the fish stocks in the ocean are dangerously low; how many people are in what kinds of work, what companies are trading and whether economic activity is expanding.

To know all this and more involves a systematic effort of finding out. It means seeking out high-quality data that can be used to compare outcomes and changes over time and between and within countries, and con- tinuing to do so, year after year. It means careful planning, spending money on technical expertise, robust systems, and ever-changing technologies. It means making data available, building public trust in the data, and expanding people's ability to use it, so that their needs are at the heart of these processes.

Since 2000, the effort involved in monitoring the Millennium Development Goals (MDGs) has spurred increased investment to improve data for monitoring and accountability. As a result, more is known now about the state of the world and, particularly, the poorest people in it. But despite this significant progress, huge data and knowledge gaps remain about some of the biggest challenges we face, and many people and groups still go uncounted.

These gaps limit governments' ability to act and to communicate honestly with the public. Months into the Ebola outbreak, for example, it is still hard to know how many people have died, or where.

And now the stakes are rising. In 2015, the world will embark on an even more ambitious initiative, a new development agenda underpinned by the Sustainable Development Goals (SDGs). Achieving these goals will require integrated action on social, environmental and economic challenges, with a focus on inclusive, participatory development that leaves no one behind. This in turn will require another significant increase in the data and information that is available to individuals, governments, civil society, companies and international organisations to plan, monitor and be held accountable for their actions. A huge increase in the capacity of many governments, institutions and individuals will be needed to deliver and use this data.

Fortunately, this challenge comes together with a huge opportunity

THE GROWTH OF DATA : TRENDS IN DATA AVAILABILITY, DATA OPENNESS AND MOBILE PHONE USE

Number of surveys registered by the International Household Survey Network, by year in which data collection was finished

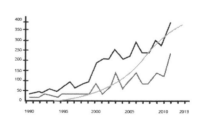

SOURCE: * INTERNATIONAL HOUSEHOLD SURVEY NETWORK (HTTP://CATALOG.IHSN.ORG/INDEX.PHP/CATALOG). FOR A DETAILED ANALYSIS OF GLOBAL TRENDS IN SURVEY DATA AVAILABILITY, SEE, E.G., DEMOMBYNES AND SANDEFUR (2014), " COSTING A DATA REVOLUTION," CENTER FOR GLOBAL DEVELOPMENT, WORKING PAPER 383.
** WORLD BANK (HTTP://DATA.WORLDBANK.ORG/INDICATOR/IT.CEL.SETS.P2). BASED ON DATA FROM THE INTERNATIONAL TELECOMMUNICATION UNION (ITU), WORLD TELECOMMUNICATION/ICT INDICATORS DATABASE

The volume of data in the world is increasing exponentially: one estimate has it that 90% of the data in the world has been created in the last two years.[i] As the graph above demonstrates, the volumes of both traditional sources of data (represented by the number of household surveys registered) and new sources (mobile subscriptions per 100 people) have been rising, and openness is increasing (numbers of surveys placed online).

Thanks to new technologies, the volume, level of detail, and speed of data available on societies, the economy and the environment is without precedent. Governments, companies, researchers and citizens groups are in a ferment of experimentation, innovation and adaptation to the new world of data. People, economies and societies are adjusting to a world of faster, more networked and more comprehensive data – and all the fears and dangers, as well as opportunities, that brings.

This is the "data revolution": the opportunity to improve the data that is essential for decision-making, accountability and solving development challenges. This report calls on governments and the UN to act to enable data to play its full role in the realisation of sustainable development by closing key gaps in access and use of data: between developed and developing countries, between information-rich and information-poor people, and between the private and public sectors.

This report has been prepared in response to a request by the Secretary-General of the United Nations. We hope it will also be helpful to Member States, the UN System as a whole, and to the large constituencies that support the three pillars of the UN: peace, human rights and development.

Revolutions begin with people, not with reports, and the data revolution is no different. This report is not about how to create a data revolution – it is already happening – but how to mobilise it for sustainable development. It is an urgent call for action to support the aspiration for sustainable development and avert risks, stop and reverse growing inequalities in access to data and information, and ensure that the promise of the data revolution is realised for all.

DEFINING THE DATA REVOLUTION

Since the phrase was coined in may 2013 in the report of the high-level panel of eminent persons on the post-2015 development agenda, the "data revolution" has come to mean many things to many people. Here, we take it to mean the following:

The data revolution is:

- an explosion in the volume of data, the speed with which data are produced, the number of producers of data, the dissemination of data, and the range of things on which there is data, coming from new technologies such as mobile phones and the "internet of things", and from other sources, such as qualitative data, citizen-generated data and perceptions data;

- a growing demand for data from all parts of society.

The data revolution for sustainable development is:

- the integration of these new data with traditional data to produce high-quality information that is more detailed, timely and relevant for many purposes and users, especially to foster and monitor sustainable development;

- the increase in the usefulness of data through a much greater degree of openness and transparency, avoiding invasion of privacy and abuse of human rights from misuse of data on individuals and groups, and minimising inequality in production, access to and use of data;

- ultimately, more empowered people, better policies, better decisions and greater participation and accountability, leading to better outcomes for people and the planet

MINIMISING THE RISKS AND MAXIMISING THE OPPORTUNITIES OF THE DATA REVOLUTION

As with any change, the data revolution comes with a range of new risks, posing questions and challenges concerning the access to and use of data, and threatening a growing inequality in access to and use of information. These risks must be addressed.

Fundamental elements of human rights have to be safeguarded: privacy, respect for minorities or data sovereignty requires us to balance the rights of individuals with the benefits of the collective. Much of the new data is collected passively, from the 'digital footprints' people leave behind, from sensor-enabled objects or is inferred via algorithms.

The growing gap between the data people actively offer and the amounts of "massive and passive" data being generated and mediated by third parties fuels anxiety among individuals and communities.

Some of this is well-founded. As more is known about people and the environment, there is a correspondingly greater risk that the data could be used to harm, rather than to help. People could be harmed in material ways, if the huge amount that can be known about people's movements, their likes and dislikes, their social interactions and relationships is used with malicious intent, such as hacking into bank accounts or discriminating in access to services. People and societies can be harmed in less material, but nonetheless real ways if individuals are embarrassed or suffer social isolation as a result of information becoming public.

There is a longer-term cost if a breakdown in trust between people and the institutions that have access to their data means that people do not feel confident giving consent to uses of their data for the social good, such as to track patterns of disease or assess inequalities.

People and the planet could also be harmed inadvertently, if data that have not been checked for quality are used for policy or decision-making and turn out to be wrong.

There is also a risk of growing inequality. Major gaps are already opening up between the data haves and have-nots. Without action, a whole new inequality frontier will open up, splitting the world between those who know, and those who do not. Many people are excluded from the new world of data and information by language, poverty, lackof education, lack of technology infrastructure, remoteness or prejudice and discrimination. While the use of new technologies has exploded everywhere in the last ten years, the costs are still prohibitive for many. In Nicaragua, Bolivia and Honduras,for example, the price of a mobile broadband subscription exceeds 10% of average monthly GDP per capita, compared to France and the Republic of Korea where it is less than 0.1%.[ii] The information society should not force a choice between food and knowledge.

In several countries, the public sector is not keeping up with companies, which are increasingly able to collect, analyse and respond to real-time data as quickly as it is generated. Richer countries are benefitting more from the new possibilities than poorer countries that lack the resources for investment, training and experimentation. According to McKinsey, African countries spend about 1.1% of GDP on investment in and use of internet services, less than a third of what, on average, is spent by richer countries – meaning that the gap in internet availability and use is growing every year, as some regions accelerate ahead.[iii] The graph below shows how advanced economies are ahead of the rest of the world on almost every indicator of access to, use of, and impact of the use of digital technologies.

THIS IS THE REVOLUTION

As part of a project to engage young people in disaster risk reduction, teenagers in Rio de Janeiro have used cameras attached to kites to gather aerial images, helping to identify the presence or absence of drainage systems, the availability of sanitation facilities, and potential impediments to evacuation. In Rio, this has already led to the removal of piled-up garbage and the repair of a bridge.

Source: UNICEF (http://www.unicef.org/statistics/brazil_62043.html)

INEQUALITIES IN ACCESS TO AND USE OF ICT SERVICES*

Number of surveys registered by the International Household Survey Network, by year in which data collection was finished

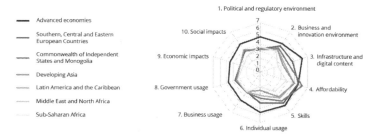

— Advanced economies

— Southern, Central and Eastern European Countries

···· Commonwealth of Independent States and Mongolia

···· Developing Asia

···· Latin America and the Caribbean

···· Middle East and North Africa

···· Sub-Saharan Africa

* REGIONAL SCORE AVERAGES BASED ON THE GLOBAL INFORMATION TECHNOLOGY REPORT 2013, BY THE WORLD ECONOMIC FORUM

We believe that the data revolution can be a revolution for equality. More, and more open, data can help ensure that knowledge is shared, creating a world of informed and empowered citizens, capable of holding decision-makers accountable for their actions. There are huge opportunities before us and change is already happening.

But if our vision is of a world where data and information reduce rather than increase inequalities, we are still a long way from realising that ambition. Without deliberate actions, the opportunities will be slower in coming and more unequally distributed when they arrive, and the risks will be greater.

It is up to governments to put in place the rules and systems to realise this vision, working with domestic stakeholders and in the multilateral system, at regional and global levels. Governments, through the legal systems they enforce, are the ultimate guarantors of the public good. If the new world of data is to be based on public trust and public consent, there has to be a confidence that governments can and will play this role, at least in part through the creation and enforcement of new rules. It is governments – ideally work- ing in collaboration with forward looking and socially responsible private institutions, civil society and academia – that can set and enforce legal frameworks to guarantee data privacy and security of data for individuals, and ensure its quality and inde- pendence. It is governments that can balance public and private interests and create systems that foster incentives without creating unacceptable inequali- ties, adopt frameworks for safe and responsible use and manage the international system that can transfer finance and techni- cal expertise to bring the least informed people and institutions up to the level of the most informed. And it is governments that are elected to respond to citizens on their choices and priorities.

THIS IS THE REVOLUTION

Indonesian authorities estimated that 50,000 people in Sumatra suffered from respiratory illness as a result of forest fires in March 2014. Several major cities were effectively closed for weeks. the environmental impacts were equally severe, with valuable forest and peat land burned, contributing significantly to Indonesia's greenhouse gas emissions. the immediate availability of free forest fire data on the World Resources institute (WRi)'s global forest Watch site (gfW) enabled companies – asia pulp and paper (app) and asia pacific Resources limited (apRil),Indonesia's two largest pulp and paper producers – to evaluate daily where their limited resources are best deployed to respond to fires on lands they are responsible for the governments of Singapore and Indonesia also used gfW-fires' ultra–high resolution imagery, available through a partnership with Digital globe, to crack down on illegal burning by companies. And gfW-fires, combined with the Indonesian government's Karhutla (land and forest fires) Monitoring system, enabled firefighters to reduce response time from 36 hours to 4 hours. Source: World Resources Institute (http://www.wri.org/our-work/project/global-forest-watch)

WE BELIEVE THAT THE DATA REVOLUTION CAN BE A REVOLUTION FOR EQUALITY

New institutions, new actors, new ideas and new partnerships are needed, and all have something to offer the data revolution. National statistical offices, the traditional guardians of public data for the public good, will remain central to the whole of government efforts to harness the data revolution for sustainable development. To fill this role, however, they will need to change, and more quickly than in the past, and continue to adapt, abandoning expensive and cumbersome production processes, incorporating new data sources, including administrative data from other government departments, and focusing on providing data that is human and machine-readable, compatible with geospatial information systems and available quickly enough to ensure that the data cycle matches the decision cycle. In many cases, technical and financial investments will be needed to enable those changes to happen, and strong collaboration between public institutions and the private sector can help official agencies to jump straight to new technologies and ways of doing things.

NEW DATA, HEALTH SERVICES AND MALARIA

Malaria is one of the biggest killers in several developing countries and imposes a huge strain on health systems. Using new data sources to inform planning and policy can improve services and reduce deaths.

The Mtrac programme in uganda,[iv] supported by uniCef, the WHO and USAID, uses SMS surveys completed by health workers to alert public health officials to outbreaks of malaria, and lets them know how much medicine is on hand at health facilities, so they can anticipate and resolve any shortages. Before Mtrac, the Ministry of Health had very little health facility-level data, either paper or electronic. By March 2014, thanks to this programme, about 1,200 district health officials, 18,700 health facility workers, and 7,400 village health team workers were using the system. Now the Ugandan government is collecting data from thousands of health facilities, capturing and analysing results within 48 hours at a total cost of less than US$150 per poll. The anonymous hotline receives on average more than 350 actionable reports per month, and approximately 70% of these reports are successfully fol- lowed up at the district level within 2 weeks. The number of facilities that are out of stock of artemisinin-based Combination therapies (aCts) to treat malaria at any given time has fallen from 80% to 15%.

Research in Cote d'Ivoire shows how, in the longer term, new sources of data might also have a role in tracking and predicting epidemics of malaria or other diseases.

Combining strongly anonymised data on communication patterns from the Orange mobile telephone network with information on the spread of malaria from the WHO, the University of Minnesota school of public health produced epidemiological models that are more detailed than any currently in use. This knowledge could be used to create services to notify doctors, field hospitals and the general public ahead of epidemics, using mobile networks or local radio. Similar work has been done on the spread of AIDS, cholera and meningitis, and could, if the data is made available, be used for rapid response and planning for new epidemics.

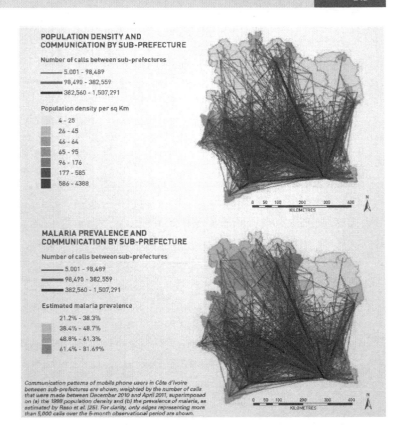

POPULATION DENSITY AND COMMUNICATION BY SUB-PREFECTURE

Number of calls between sub-prefectures

- 5.001 - 98,489
- 98,490 - 382,559
- 382,560 - 1,507,291

Population density per sq Km

- 4 - 25
- 26 - 45
- 46 - 64
- 65 - 95
- 96 - 176
- 177 - 585
- 586 - 4388

MALARIA PREVALENCE AND COMMUNICATION BY SUB-PREFECTURE

Number of calls between sub-prefectures

- 5.001 - 98,489
- 98,490 - 382,559
- 382,560 - 1,507,291

Estimated malaria prevalence

- 21.2% - 38.3%
- 38.4% - 48.7%
- 48.8% - 61.3%
- 61.4% - 81.69%

Communication patterns of mobile phone users in Côte d'Ivoire between sub-prefectures are shown, weighted by the number of calls that were made between December 2010 and April 2011, superimposed on (a) the 1998 population density and (b) the prevalence of malaria, as estimated by Raso et al. [25]. For clarity, only edges representing more than 5,000 calls over the 5-month observational period are shown.

2   THE DATA REVOLUTION FOR SUSTAINABLE DEVELOPMENT

In september 2015, the UN member states are expected to commit to an ambitious new set of global goals for a new era of sustainable development. Achieving them will require an unprecedented joint effort on the part of governments at every level, civil society and the private sector, and millions of individual choices and actions. To be realised, the SDGs will require a monitoring and accountability framework and a plan for implementation. A commitment to realise the opportunities of the data revolution should be firmly embedded into the action plan for the SDGs, to support those countries most in need of resources, and to set the world on track for an unprecedented push towards a new world of data for change.

Why a data revolution for sustainable development?

Although there have been steady and dramatic improvements in recent decades, there is still work to do to create a clearer and more up-to-date picture of the world, to use in planning, monitoring and evaluation of the policies and programmes that will together achieve the SDGs, and in holding to account those in positions of power over resources and other decisions that affect people's lives.
 There are two main problems to address:

- **Not enough high-quality data.** In a world increasingly awash with data, it is shock- ing how little is known about some people and some parts of our environment. The world has made huge strides in recent years in tracking specific aspects of human development such as poverty, nutrition, child and maternal health and access to water and sanitation. However, too many countries still have poor data, data arrives too late and too many issues are still barely covered by existing data. For example, in several countries data on employment are notoriously unreliable, data on age and disability are routinely not collected and a great deal of data is difficult to access to citizens or is not available until several years have passed since the time of collection.

Percentage of MDG data

Currently available for developing countries by nature of source*

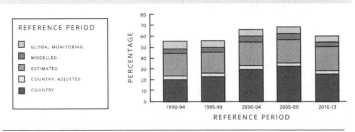

PERCENTAGE OF MDG DATA CURRENTLY AVAILABLE FOR DEVELOPING COUNTRIES BY NATURE OF SOURCE

REFERENCE PERIOD

- GLOBAL MONITORING
- MODELLED
- ESTIMATED
- COUNTRY, ADJUSTED
- COUNTRY

Availability is defined as the proportion of country-indicator combinations that have at least one data observation within the reference period. figures are based on 55mdg core indicators, as of october 2014

The figure above presents a summary snapshot of current data availability in the MDG database (as of October 2014), covering 55 core indicators for 157 developing countries or areas. There, a country is counted as having data for an indicator if it has at least one observation over the reference period, and availability is broken down by whether the data comes from country or international data sources,
and whether it is estimated, adjusted or modelled.[vi] Overall, the picture is improving though still poor, so there is no five-year period when the availability of data is more than 70% of what is required. The drop in data availability after 2010 demonstrates the extent of the time lags that persist between collection and release of data. There is considerable variation in data availability between indicators, where, for example, data on malaria indicators is very scarce, while for the ratio of girls to boys enrolled in primary, secondary and tertiary education there is relatively good country level data available for most

countries and years (though much remains to be done in tracking other indicators essential to monitoring educational outcomes).

THIS IS THE REVOLUTION

As part of the development of their National Strategy for the Development Of Statistics (NSDS) completed in partnership with the partnership in statistics for development in the 21st century (PARIS21), Rwanda identified some simple, yet systematic, improvements that could dramatically help make better use of evidence for policy making. One innovation included moving up the publishing date of the Consumer Price Index by five days each month in response to needs from both policy makers and businesses. The release date of the demographic and health survey and living conditions survey was changed so that the information could be used in measuring Rwanda's first poverty reduction strategy and so the information could inform planning for the next one. These changes in data scheduling increased the usefulness of the data and allowed for better evidence-based decisions to be made.

Source: PARIS21 (http://www.cgdev.org/blog/better-data-rwanda)

If data availability is still low for some individual indicators and/ or countries, the graph below highlights how, when looked at from a country level, there has been a tremendous improvement in the ability of national statistical systems to provide data directly over the past ten years. This has been one of the greatest achievements of MDG monitoring, and is testament to the tremendous efforts of many national and international organisations.

Beyond the MDG indicators, other disturbing gaps exist. Entire groups of people and key issues remain invisible. Indigenous populations and slum dwellers for instance, are consistently left out of most data sets. It is still impossible to know with certainty how many disabled children are in school.

Globally, the fact of birth has not been recorded for nearly 230 million children under age five. In 2012 alone, 57 million infants – four out of every ten babies delivered worldwide that year – were not registered with civil authorities.[vii] Violence against children is often under-reported, leading to failures to protect vulnerable children.
Data is often insufficiently disaggregated at sub-national level, making it hard for policy makers or communities to compare their progress with that of other communities or the country as a whole. In water supply, for example, the analysis of many household surveys produces a single national estimate of access to clean and safe water in rural areas, but does not show how it varies between districts.

Increase over time in number of mdg indicator series for which trend analysis was possible for developing countries*

INCREASE OVER TIME IN NUMBER OF MDG INDICATOR SERIES FOR WHICH TREND ANALYSIS WAS POSSIBLE FOR DEVELOPING COUNTRIES

NO. OF INDICATOR SERIES WITH
AT LEAST TWO DATA POINTS:

- 0-5
- 6-10
- 11-15
- 15-22

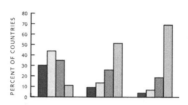

 # Figures are based on a subset of 22 MDG indicators.
Source: Updated figures based on United Nations, " Indicators for monitoring the Millennium Development Goals," Report of the Secretary-General,45th Session of the United Nations Statistical COmission, 4-7 Mar, 2014. (E/CN. 3/2014/29).

Gender inequality and the undervaluing of women's activities and priorities in every sphere has been replicated in the statistical record. Many of the issues of most concern to women are poorly served by existing data; just over half of all countries report data on intimate partner violence, and where it is reported quality is not consistent, data is rarely collected from women over 49, and data are not comparable.[viii] Very little data is available on the distribution of money or the division of labour within households. Much more data are needed on the economic roles of women of all ages as caregivers to children, older persons and the disabled in the house- hold and in the labour force. Of the 42.9 million persons of concern to the United Nations High Commissioner for Refugees

(UNHCR) globally at the end of 2013, sex composition was known for only 56 percent of the population, that no groups are excluded, and with an unprecedented level of detail.

- Data that are not used or not usable. To be useful, data must be of high quality, at a level of disaggregation that is appropriate to the issue at hand, and must be made accessible to those who want or need to use them. Too many countries still have data that are of insufficient quality to be useful in making decisions, holding governments to account or fostering innovation. Good data are relevant, accurate, timely, accessible, comparable and produced free of political interferences.

- Comparability and standardisation are crucial, as they allow data from different sources or time periods to be combined, and the more data can be combined, the more useful they are. Combining data allows for changes of scale – e.g., aggregating data from different countries to produce regional or global figures. It allows for comparison over time, if data on the same thing collected at different moments can be brought together to reveal trends. But too much data is still produced using different standards – household surveys that ask slightly different questions or geospatial data that uses different geographical definitions. There is, for example, no standard definition of an "urban" area. And too little data are available at a level of disaggregation that is appropriate to policy makers trying to make decisions about local-level allocation or monitoring equitable outcomes across regions. This prevents researchers, policy makers, companies or NGOs from realising the full value of the data produced. Access, too, is often restricted behind technical and/or legal barriers, or restricted by governments or companies that fear too much transparency, all of which prevent or limit effective use of data. Data buried in pdf documents, for example, are much harder for potential users to work with; administrative data that are not transferred to statistical offices; data generated by the private sector or by academic researchers that are never released or data released too late to be useful; data that cannot be translated into action because of lack of operational tools to leverage them. This is a huge loss in terms of the benefits that could be gained from more open data and from being able to link data across different sectors. Data needs to be generated with users in mind. Too often data providers underinvest in identifying and engaging those in a position to use data to drive action. Agencies with a mandate to collect public information are not always well-suited to ensuring their information is used by stakeholders, while civil society and the private sector could play a critical role in translating data into a form that is more readily useable.

THIS IS THE REVOLUTION

In Mexico, a budget research and advocacy group called Fundar developed an online database of government farm subsidies. one of the problems brought to light was the way in which billions of dollars of the funds were distributed. Though many farm subsidy programs claim to target the neediest farmers, the database revealed that a small group of wealthy farmers had captured the vast majority of subsidy funds over time (the top 10 percent of recipients had received over 50 percent of the funds). The studies contributed to the government decision to review and change the distribution of the subsidies.

The data we want for sustainable development

Too much that needs to be known remains unknown. Data could be used better to improve lives and increase the power and control that citizens have over their destinies. Data is a resource, an endless source of fuel for innovation that will power sustainable development, of which we must learn to become effective and responsible stewards. Like any resource, it must be managed for the public good, and to ensure that the benefits flow to all people and not just the few. Data must be available, and must be turned into the information that can be confidently used by people to understand and improve their lives and the world around them.

The world we need, if the data we have is to be used to the fullest to achieve sustainable development, is a world of data that is transformed in the following ways:

- **Data for everyone.** The rules, systems and investments that underpin how official data is collected and and managed should be focused on the needs of people, while protecting their rights as the producers of that information. These data, and the information produced from them, should reflect what is important to people and the constraints and opportunities that affect their lives. This process should include all people – leaving no one out, and disaggregating in ways that allow the relevant differences and similarities between people and groups to be reflected in analysis and policy. Rules and standards should be aimed at reducing information inequalities and providing the highest-quality information for all, in the most easily understood format. The priority should always be to use data and information to improve outcomes, experiences and possibilities for people in the short and long term.[x] When the data is not confidential, it should be available and useable as open data. There must be respect for privacy and personal ownership of personal data, and mechanisms in place so that people themselves have access to the information and are able to make choices accordingly. Crucially, people must have means for redress if they feel that they are being harmed or their rights infringed by the use of their data.

- **Data for now.** If data is to be useful and support good decision-making, it has to be ready at the time when decisions are being made or where the opportunity for influencing the outcomes is there. Trade-offs between timeliness and other quality dimensions depend on the purpose to which data is being put. New technologies and innovations provide the opportunity for the public sector, citizens groups, individuals and companies to have access to data that, with due regard for privacy, security and human rights, is aligned with their own decision- making cycles and information needs – available when and how they want it – and strengthen policy planning, crisis early warning, programme operations, service delivery, impact evaluation, and disaster response.[xi]

- **Data for the future.** Data are a key resource not just for decision-making now but for future modelling and problem solving. It is almost impossible to precisely predict future needs, or know how current data could be re-used in the service of complex and interconnected problems as yet unknown or unsolved. Data at different timescales will be most useful for solving future problems if they are part of a flexible and connected system, not tied to one project or research question. Data that can be re-used at different scales, and combined with other data, can better reflect the complex and dynamic interactions between people and the planet. We need to begin investing in data today as a shared resource that will enable the innovations required to meet the challenges of tomorrow

OUR VISION FOR THE FUTURE

By 2020, we hope to be witnessing the emergence of a vibrant "global data ecosystem" to support the monitoring and implementation of the SDGs and in which:

- **Governments** empower public institutions, including statistical offices, protecting their independence, to take on the needed changes to respond to the data revolution and put in place regulatory frameworks that ensure robust data privacy and data protection, and promote the release of data as open data by all data producers, and build capacity for continuous data innovation

- **Governments, international and regional institutions and donors** invest in data, providing resources to countries and regions where statistical or technical capacity is weak; develop infrastructures and implement standards to continuously improve and maintain data quality and usability; keep data open and usable by all. They also finance analytical research in forward-looking and experimental   subjects.

- **International and regional** organisations work with other stakeholders to set and enforce common standards for data collection, production, anonymisation, sharing and use to ensure that new data flows are safely and ethically transformed into global public goods, and maintain a system of quality control and audit for all systems and all data producers and users. They also support countries in their capacity-building efforts.

- **Statistical systems** are empowered, resourced and independent, to quickly adapt to the new world of data to collect, process, disseminate and use high-quality, open, disaggregated and geo-coded data, both quantitative and qualitative. They may be less about producing data and more about managing and curating data and information created outside of their organisations.

- **All public, private and civil society data producers** share data and the methods used to process them, according to globally, regionally, or nationally brokered agreements and norms. They publish data, geospatial information and statistics in open formats and with open terms of use, following global common principles and technical standards, to maintain quality and openness and protect privacy.

- **Governments, civil society, academia and the philanthropic** sector work together to raise awareness of publicly available data, to strengthen the data and statistical literacy ("numeracy") of citizens, the media, and other "infomediaries", ensuring that all people have capacity to input into and evaluate the quality of data and use them for their own decisions, as well as to fully participate in initiatives to foster citizenship in the information age.

- **The private sector** reports on its activities using common global standards for integrating data on its economic, environmental and human-rights activities and impacts, building on and strengthening the collaboration already established among institutions that set standards for business reporting. Some companies also cooperate with the public sector, according to agreed and sustainable business models, in the production of statistical data for SDGs monitoring and other public purposes.

- **Civil society organisations** and individuals hold governments and companies accountable using evidence on the impact of their actions, provide feedback to data producers, develop data literacy and help communities and individuals to generate and use data, to ensure accountability and make better decisions for themselves.

- **The media** fairly report on the statistical and scientific evidence available on relevant dimensions of sustainable development and foster an evidence-based public discourse using advanced visualisation technologies to better communicate key data to people.

- **Academics and scientists** carry out analyses based on data coming from multiple sources providing long-term perspectives, knowledge and data resources to guide sustainable development at global, regional, national, and local scales. They make demographic and scientific data as open as possible for public and private use in sustainable development; provide feedback and independent advice and expertise to support accountability and more effective decision-making, and provide leadership in education, outreach, and capacity building efforts.

PROGRESS TOWARD UNIVERSAL CIVIL REGISTRATION AND VITAL STATISTICS (CRVS)

One of the most fundamental inequalities is between those who are counted and those who are not. Millions of people of all ages in low- and middle-income countries are denied basic services and protection of their rights because they are absent from official records. Lacking records of their birth and civil status, they are excluded from health coverage, schooling, social protection programs, and humanitarian response in emergencies and conflicts. A well-functioning CRVS system is essential to overcome this injustice. It is also vital for policy making and for monitoring, generating statistics for policy formulation, planning and implementation, and monitoring of population dynamics and health indicators on a continuous basis at the national and local level. These data help to identify inequalities in access to services and differences in outcomes. They also improve the quality of other statistics, such as household surveys, that depend on accurate demographic benchmarks. One proven solution is through issuance of a digital identity, which gives government and business the ability to deliver citizen services electronically, boosting efficiency and driving innovation and serving people, often in isolated areas.

Despite progress in recent years, many countries still lack the capacity, infrastructure, and resources to implement well-functioning CRVS systems. The good news is that international partners and countries have recently agreed on a CRVS scaling up investment plan[xv] . The plan covers activities over a 10-year period from 2015 to 2024, with the goal of universal civil registration of births, deaths, marriages, and other vital events, including cause of death, and access to legal proof of registration for all individuals by 2030. Africa and Asia have already established regional programs to motivate political support, systematic national planning, and provision of technical assistance. and key donors[xvi] announced recently the establishment of a trust fund to support developing countries' plans to establish CRVS systems with the aim of accelerating progress toward the health-related Sustainable Development Goals.

MOBILISING THE DATA REVOLUTION FOR SUSTAINABLE DEVELOPMENT: A CALL TO ACTION

A revolution is an idea – an inspiring vision of a world of fast-flowing data deployed for the public good, and of citizens and governments excited and empowered by the possibilities this creates. But it is also a practical proposition. Getting from here to there involves deliberate actions and choices.

Decisive action now, taking advantage of the current political opportunities, can set the scene and have a positive impact for years to come. Achieving the SDGs demands embracing the data revolution. We urge the UN Member States and system organisations to dramatically speed up their work in this field to support the global aspiration for sustainable development.

Data will be one of the fundamental elements of the accountability framework for the SDGs. Having high-quality data, and using it to create information that can track progress, monitor the use of resources, and evaluate the impacts of policy and programmes on different groups, is a key ingredient in creating more mutually accountable and participatory structures to monitor the new goals. However, we recognise that data is not the whole story. This report is about how data, and information, can be improved and made more accessible. The decisions on how those data and information will be used in any specific accountability framework for the SDGs belongs to the UN Member States and, as such, remains beyond the scope of this report.

Our recommendations for how to mobilise the data revolution for sustainable development suggest a comprehensive programme of action in four areas, illustrated to the right:

- principles and standards,
- technology, innovation and analysis,
- capacity and resources,
- leadership and governance.,

At the heart of the recommendations in every area are people and the planet – our revolution is with them and for them.

Principles and standards

One of the key roles of the UN and other international or regional organisations is setting principles and standards to guide collective actions within a global community and according to common norms. We believe that mobilising the data revolution for achieving sustainable development urgently requires such a standard setting, building on existing initiatives in various domains.

We recommend ...

... that the UN develop a comprehensive strategy and a roadmap towards a new 'Global Consensus on Data', building upon existing efforts in other domains, setting principles and agreeing standards to build trust and enable cooperation, including

- **Agree on and promote adoption of specific principles related to the data revolution**, drawing from and building upon those described in the next two pages, to be further developed by the appropriate UN bodies and agreed by their Member States;
- **Accelerate the development and adoption of legal, technical, geospatial and statistical standards**, in a range of areas including, but not limited to:
  - Openness and exchange of data and metadata, including interoperability of data and information systems; demographic and geospatial information, including "geographic semantic" management and exchange; global exchange of information on illicit financial flows; open data and digital rights management and licensing;
  - Protection of human rights, including: standards for anonymising data that is personally identifiable, and standards and enforce- ment mechanisms for data security, integrity, documentation, preservation, and access.

BASIC PRINCIPLES FOR THE DATA REVOLUTION FOR SUSTAINABLE DEVELOPMENT

The data revolution will need to be harnessed for sustainable and inclusive development through proactive measures and guided by the following key principles:

Data quality and integrity

1   Poor quality data can mislead. The entire process of data design, collection, analysis and dissemination needs to be demonstrably of high quality and integrity. Clear standards need to be developed to safeguard quality, drawing on the UN fundamental principles of official statistics and the work of independent third parties. A robust framework for quality assurance is required, particularly for official this includes internal systems as well as periodic audits by professional and independent third parties. Existing tools for improving the quality of statistical data should be used and strengthened, and data should be classified using commonly agreed criteria and quality benchmarks.

Data disaggregation

2   No one should be invisible to the extent possible and with due safeguards for individual privacy and data quality, data should be disaggregated across many dimensions, such as geography, wealth, disability, sex and age. Disaggregated data should be collected on other dimensions based on their relevance to the program, policy or other matter under consideration, for example, ethnicity, migrant status, marital status, HIV status, sexual orientation and gender indentity, with due protections

for privacy and human rights. Disaggregated data can provide a better comparative picture of what works, and help inform and promote evidence based policy making at every level.

Data timeliness

3   Data delayed is data denied. Standards should be tightened and technology leveraged to reduce the time between the design of data collection and publication of data. The value of data produced can be enhanced by ensuring there is a steady flow of high-quality and timely data from national, international, private big data sources, and digital data generated by people. The data cycle must watch the decision cycle.

Data transparency and openness

4   Many publicly-funded datasets, as well as data on public spending and budgets, are not available to other ministries or to the general public. All data on public matters and/ or funded by public funds, including those data produced by private sector, should be made public and "open by default", with narrow exemptions for genuine security or privacy concerns. It needs to be both technically open (i.e, available in a machine-readable standard format so that it can be retrieved and meaningfully processed by a computer application) and legally open (i.e., explicitly licensed in a way that permits commercial and non-commercial use and re-use without restrictions). The underlying data design and sampling, methods, tools and datasets should be explained and published alongside findings to enable greater scrutiny, understanding and independent analysis.

Data usability and curation

5   Too often data is presented in ways that cannot be understood by most people. The data architecture should therefore place great emphasis on user-centred design and user friendly interfaces. Communities of "information intermediaries" should be fostered to develop new tools that can translate raw data into information for a broader constituency of non-technical potential users and enable citizens and other data users to provide feedback.

Data protection and privacy

6.   As more data becomes available in disaggregated forms and data-silos become more integrated, privacy issues are increasingly a concern about what data is collected and how it is used. Further risk arises where collectors of big data do not have sufficient protection from demands from state bodies or interference from hackers. Clear international norms and robust national policy and legal frameworks need to be developed that regulate opt-in and opt-out, data mining, use, re-use for other purpose, transfer and dissemination. They should enable citizens to better understand and control their own data, and protect data producers from demands of governments and attacks by hackers, while still allowing for rich innovation in re-use of data for the public good. Within the agreed privacy constraints, people's rights to freedom of expression using data should be protected. People who correctly provide, collect , curate and analyse data need freedom to operate and protection from recrimination.

Data governance and independence

7   Many national statistical offices lack sufficient capacity and
     funding, and remain vulnerable to political and interest
     group influence (including by donors). Data quality should
     be protected and improved by strengthening nsos, and
     ensuring they are functionally autonomous, independent of
     sector ministries and plotical influence. Their transparency
     and accountability should be improved, including their direct
     communication with the public they serve. This can include
     independent monitoring of the same public services, for
     example, or monitoring of related indicators such as public
     satisfaction with services.

Data resources and capacity

8   There is a global responsibility to ensure that all countries have
     an effective national statistical system, capable of producing
     high-quality statistics in line with global standards and
     expectations. This requires investments in human capital, new
     technology, infrastructure, geospatial data and management
     systems in both governmental and independent systems, as
     well as information intermediaries. At the same time, national
     capacity for data science must be developed to leverage
     opportunities in big data, to complement high-quality official
     statistics. increased domestic resources and international
     support for devel- oping countries are needed to have the data
     revolution contribute to sustainable development. applications
     of big data for the public good must be developed and scaled
     up transparently, demonstrating full compliance with applicable
     laws.

Data rights

9   Human rights cut across many issues related to the data revolution. These rights include but are not limited to the right to be counted, the right to an identity, the right to privacy and to ownership of personal data, the right to due process (for example when data is used as evidence in proceedings, or in administrative descisions), freedom of expression, the right to participation, the right to non- discrimination and equality, and principles of consent. any legal or regulatory mechanisms, or networks or partner- ships, set up to mobilise the data revolution for sustainable development should have the protection of human rights as a core part of their activities, specify who is respon- sible for upholding those rights, and should support the protection, respect and fulfilment of human rights.

STRENGTHENING NATIONAL CAPACITIES WILL BE THE ESSENTIAL TEST OF ANY DATA REVOLUTION

Technology, innovation and analysis

Technology has been and will continue to be a fundamental driver of the data revolution. To harness the benefits of new technology, large and continuing investments in innovation are required at all levels, but especially in those institutions which are currently lagging behind. In addition, but beyond the scope of this report, an urgent effort needs to be made to increase access to information technologies by, among other things, increasing access to broadband, increasing literacy, including adult literacy, and increasing the use of ICT in schools worldwide, to ensure that all people, including the poorest, have access to the technologies that can improve their lives.

We recommend ...

... that the UN foster the establishment of a "Network of Data Innovation Networks" for sustainable development bringing together a range of partners and existing networks to generate knowledge and solve common problems. Some specific areas of activity could be:

- **Urgently leverage emerging data sources for SDG monitoring, through an 'SDG data lab'**: The lab should mobilise key public, private and civil society data providers, academics and stakeholders to identify available and missing data and indicators, as well as opportunities for benefitting from new methods, analytical tools and technologies to improve the coverage, timeliness and availability of indicators in each of the SDG areas. Drawing on the existing MDG monitoring architecture, and working with other networks such as the Sustainable Development Solutions Network, it would develop new methodologies for monitoring new goals from January 2016

- **Develop systems for global data sharing:** Identify areas where the development of common infrastructures to exploit the data revolution for sustainable development could solve capacity problems, produce efficiencies and encourage collaborations. One such suggestion would be a "world statistics cloud", to store metadata produced by different institutions but according to common standards, rules and specifications.

- **Fill research gaps:** Identify critical research gaps, such as the relationships between data, incentives and behaviour. Engage research centres, innovators and governments in the development of publicly available data analytics tools and alogrithms to better capture and evaluate long-term trends affecting sustainable development.

- **Create incentives:** Engage social entrepreneurs, private sector, academia, media, civil society and other individuals and institutions in this global effort through initiatives such as prizes and data challenges.

Capacity and resource

Strengthening national capacities in all areas from data production to use will be the essential test of any data revolution, in particular in developing countries where the basic infrastructure is often lacking. Monitoring a new and expanded set of Sustainable Development Goals will not be possible in many countries without new and sustained investment, so urgent mobilisation of new funds is needed.

We recommend ...

... that a proposal be developed for a new funding stream and innovative financing mechanisms to support the data revolution for sustainable development, for discussion at the "Third International Conference on Financing for Development", which will take place in Addis Ababa in July 2015. The proposal should be built on the following five pillars:

- **Investment needs:** An analysis of the scale of investments needed for the establishment of a modern system to monitor progress towards SDGs, especially in developing countries. This analysis, building on various attempts currently ongoing, should highlight the costs as well as opportunities for efficiency gains associated with different production systems. Particular attention should be paid to the need for investment in data to analyse the challenges facing the very poorest people and communities, and to involve them as users of data.

- **Managing funds:** A proposal on how to manage and monitor new funding for the data revolution for sustainable development, taking stock of existing sources and forms of funding. This should look at how funding from a range of sources could be used most effectively, and managed and disbursed in line with national priorities to incentivise innovation, collaboration and whole systems approaches, while also encouraging creativity and experimentation and accepting that not all initiatives will succeed.

- **Private sector participation:** A proposal on how to leverage the resources and creativity of the private sector, including an examination of suggestions for creating incentives for the private sector to invest given companies' expectations of time horizon and returns.
- **Capacity development:** A proposal to improve existing arrangements for fostering the necessary capacity development and technology transfer. This should include upgrading the "National Strategies for the Development of Statistics" (NSDS) to do better at coordinated and long-term planning, and in identifying sound investments and engaging non-official data producers in a cooperative effort to speed up the production, dissemination and use of data, strengthening civil society's

capacity and resources to produce, use and disseminate data.

- **Global data literacy:** A proposal for a special investment to increase global data literacy. To close the gap between people able to benefit from data and those who cannot, in 2015 the UN should work with other organisations to develop an education program and promote new learning approaches to improve people's, infomediaries' and public servants' data literacy. Special efforts should be made to reach people living in poverty through dedicated programmes.

Governance and leadership

Strong leadership by the UN is vital to make the data revolution serve sustainable development. Such leadership should be made very concrete through various actions and activities, and the continuous engagement of all rel- evant partners, maintaining a very open and transparent approach with governments, the private sector, NGOs, the media, and academic researchers. The primary aim would be to add value to existing institutional setups, accelerating the delivery of their outputs and building new partnerships. Short- and medium-term results should be clearly spelled out, and periodic reviews should be undertaken to ensure that global cooperation in this area is on the right track.

We recommend ...

...the establishment of a "Global Partnership for Sustainable Development Data" (GPSDD) to mobilise and coordinate as many initiatives and institutions as possible to achieve the vision sketched above. The GPSDD could promote several initiatives, such as:

- **World Forum:** The establishment of a biennial "World Forum on Sustainable Development Data", and associated regional and country level events and ongoing engagements. These would maintain momentum on data improvements, foster regular engagement between private, public and community level data collectors and users, showcase ongoing activities and initiatives, create a network of 'data champions' around the world, and provide practical spaces for innovation, knowledge sharing, advocacy and technology transfer. The first Forum should be organ- ised by the end of 2015, once the SDGs are agreed.

- **Users forum:** Establish a "Global Forum of SDG Data Users", to ensure feedback loops between data producers, processors and users to improve the usefulness of data and information produced. It would also help the international community to set priorities and assess results achieved, and could encourage replication and experimentation with user forums at country and agency level, increasing demand for and use of data. Particular attention should be paid to how to involve poor and marginalised people and communities in the forum.

- **Partnerships and coordination:** Work in partnership with international and regional organisations, and with other initiatives looking at best practices related to public data such as the Open Government Partnership (OGP) and the G8 Open Data Charter. The aim would be to enhance coordination of work in various areas, share knowledge on SDG monitoring, and encourage good practice such as open data and harmonisation. Also, to work together on developing common legal frameworks around rights to data and information and redress from abuses of data, to work together to implement new standards once agreed, and to streamline capacity building initiatives and reduce duplicated effort, mobilising new resources.

- **Data sharing:** Broker some key global public-private partnerships with private companies and civil society organisations for data sharing. Drawing on existing efforts already underway, these would provide models for best practice, useful for national and regional bodies trying to negotiate similar arrangements, would identify incentives and constraints specific to various industries, would allow for economies of scale, and would demonstrate the value and the possibility of sharing data and collaborating between public and private sectors.

We recommend ...

... some "quick wins" on SDG data to demonstrate the feasibility of different approaches, experiment and innovate with partnerships and methods as a first step to setting up longer term initiatives. In addition to the proposed "SDG Data Lab", these could include:

- **SDGs analysis and visualisation platform:** To be launched in September 2015, using the most advanced tools and features for exploring and analysing and re-using data, and demonstrating best practices in the engagement with data users through the provision of guidance and educational resources for data re-use, building on and coordinating with other platforms in other sectors. The development of the website would also represent a laboratory for fostering private-public partnerships and community-led peer-production efforts for data collection, dissemination and visualisation. It would be continuously updated during the lifetime of the SDGs, remaining a showcase for new ideas and innovations and a source of high quality and up to date information on progress.

- **A dashboard on "the state of the world":** This would harness the richness of traditional and new data, maintain the excitement and openness of the whole SDG process, engage think-tanks, academics and NGOs as well as the whole UN family in analysing, producing, verifying and auditing data, provide a place for experimentation with methods for integrating different data sources, including qualitative data, perceptions data and citizen-generated data, and eventually produce a 'people's baseline' for new goals.

REFERENCES

REFERENCES | INTRODUCTION

1. M. Kuneva, keynote speech, Roundtable on Online Data Collection, Targeting, and Profiling, 31 Mar. 2009; http://europa.eu/rapid/pressReleasesAction. do?reference=SPEECH/09/156.

2. J. Leibowitz, "Prepared Statement of the Federal Trade Commission on Consumer Privacy," US Senate Committee on Commerce, Science, and Transportation, 27 July 2010; www.ftc.gov/os/testimony/100727consumerprivacy.pdf.

3. A. Pentland, "Reality Mining of Mobile Communications: Towards a New Deal on Data," The Global Information Technology Report 2008-2009: Mobility in a Networked World,
   5. Dutta and I. Mia, eds., World Economic Forum, 2009, pp. 75-80; www.insead. edu/v1/gitr/wef/main/fullreport/ files/Chap1/1.6.pdf.

4. World Economic Forum, Personal Data: The Emergence of a New Asset Class, 2011; www3.weforum.org/docs/WEF_ ITTC_PersonalDataNewAsset_ Report_2011.pdf.

REFERENCES | CHAPTER 2

[1.]   The White House, "National Strategy for Trusted Identities in Cyberspace: Enhancing Online Choice, Efficiency, Security, and Privacy," The White House, April 2011, available on http://www.whitehouse.gov/sites/default/files/rss viewer/ NSTICstrategy 041511.pdf.

[2.]   European Commission (2016), The General Data Protection Regulation (GDPR) (Regulation (EU) 2016/679).

[3.]   World Economic Forum, Personal Data: The Emergence of a New Asset Class, 2011, available on http://www.weforum.org/reports/ personal-data-emergence-new-asset-class.

[4.]   World Economic Forum, The future of financial infrastructure, August 2016. Available at: http://www3.weforum.org/docs/WEF_The_future_of_financial_infrastructure.pdf

[5.]   World Economic Forum, A Blueprint for Digital Identity: The Role of Financial Institutions in Building Digital Identity, http://www3.weforum.org/docs/WEF_A_Blueprint_for_Digital_Identity.pdf

[6.]   D. Shrier and A. Pentland (ed), Frontiers of Financial Technology: Expeditions in future commerce, from blockchain and digital banking to prediction markets and beyond, Publisher: Visionary Future, September 2016.

[7.]   A. Pentland, T. Reid, and T. Heibeck, Big data and Health - Revolutionizing medicine and Public Health: Report of the Big Data and Health Working Group 2013, World Innovation Summit for Health, Qatar Foundation. http://www.wish-qatar.org/app/media/382.

[8.]   A. Pentland, D. Shrier, T. Hardjono, and I. Wladawsky-Berger, Towards an Internet of Trusted Data: A New Framework for Identity and Data Sharing: Input to the Whitehouse Commission on Enhancing National Cybersecurity. MIT Connection Science. August 2016.

[9.]   G. Zyskind, G., O. Nathan, and A. Pentland. Decentralizing privacy: Using blockchain to protect personal data. In Proceedings of 2015 IEEE Symposium on Security and Privacy Workshops, 180-184.

[10.]   T Hardjono, D. Greenwood and A. Pentland, Towards a Trustworthy Digital Infrastructure for Core Identities and Personal Data Stores, ID360 Conference on Identity, University of Texas, Austin. 2013.

[11.]   The Jericho Forum, "Identity Commandments," The Open Group, 2011. Available on www.opengroup.org.

12. American Bar Association, Overview of Identity Management, ABA Identity Management Legal Task Force, May 2012, available on http://meetings.abanet. org/ webupload/commupload/ CL320041/relatedresources/ ABA-Submission-to-UNCITRAL.pdf.

13. OIX, OpenID Exchange, http://openidentityexchange.org

14. FICAM, U.S. Federal Identity, Credential and Access Management (FICAM) Program, http://info.idmanagement.gov

15. SAFE-BioPharma Association, Trust Framework Provider Services, http://www. safe-biopharma.org/SAFE_Trust_Framework.htm

16. OASIS, "Assertions and Protocols for the OASIS Security Assertion Markup Language (SAML) V2.0," http://docs.oasisopen. org/security/saml/v2.0/saml-core-2.0-os.pdf, March 2005.

17. OASIS, "Glossary for the OASIS Security Assertion Markup Language (SAML) V2.0," http://docs.oasis-open.org/security/saml/v2.0/samlglossary- 2.0-os.pdf, March 2005.

18. S. Nakamoto, Bitcoin: a Peer to Peer Electronic Cash system, https://bitcoin.org/ bitcoin.pdf.

19. Ethereum. Ethereum.org.

20. R.G. Brown, J. Carlyle, I. Grigg, M. Hearn , Corda: An Introduction, August 2016. R3, http://r3cev.com/blog/2016/8/24/the-corda-non-technical-whitepaper

21. A. Pentland, "Reality Mining of Mobile Communications: Toward a New Deal on Data," in The Global Information Technology Report 2008-2009: Mobility in a Networked World, S. Dutta and I. Mia, Eds. World Economic Forum, 2009, pp. 75–80, available on http://hd.media.mit.edu/wef_globalit.pdf.

22. Y. A. de Montjoye, S. S. Wang, and A. Pentland, "On the trusted use of large-scale personal data," IEEE Data Eng. Bull., vol. 35, no. 4, pp. 5–8, 2012.

23. Y. A. de Montjoye, J. Quoidbach, F. Robic, and A. Pentland, "Predicting personality using novel mobile phone-based metrics," in Social Computing, Behavioral-Cultural Modeling and Prediction (LCNS Vol. 7812). Springer, 2013, pp. 48–55.

24. Y. A. de Montjoye, E. Shmueli, S. Wang, and A. Pentland, "openPDS: Regaining ownership and privacy of personal data," 2013.

25. J. Pieprzyk, T. Hardjono, and J. Seberry, Fundamentals of Computer Security. Springer-Verlag, 2003.

26. D. L. Chaum, "Untraceable electronic mail, return addresses, and digital pseudonyms," Communications of the ACM, vol. 24, no. 2, pp. 84–88, February 1981.

27. S. Brands, "Untraceable off-line cash in wallets with observers," in CRYPTO'93

Proceedings of the 13th Annual International Cryptology. Springer-Verlag, 1993, pp. 302–318.

28.   S. Brands, Rethinking Public Key Infrastructures and Digital Certificates. MIT Press, 2000.

29.   J. Camenisch and E. Van Herreweghen, "Design and implementation of the IBM Idemix anonymous credential system," in Proceedings of the 9th ACM conference on Computer and communications security. ACM, 2002, pp. 21–30.

30.   E. Brickell and J. Li., Enhanced Privacy ID: a Direct Anonymous Attestation Scheme with Enhanced Revocation Capabilities. IEEE Trans on Dependable and Secure Computing, 9(3):345-360, 2012.

31.   T. Hardjono and N. Smith, "Cloud-Based Commissioning of Constrained Devices using Permissioned Blockchains", in Proceedings of the 2nd ACM International Workshop on IoT Privacy, Trust, and Security (IoTPTS 2016), May 2016.

32.   Trusted Computing Group. TPM Main Specification Version 1.2. TCG Published Specification, TCG, October 2003.

33.   T. Hardjono and N. Smith (Eds). TCG Infrastructure Reference Architecture for Interoperability (Part 1) Specification Version 1.0 Rev 1.0, June 2005. http://www.trustedcomputinggroup.org/ resources.

34.   Microsoft. U-Prove Cryptographic Specification v1.1, (Rev 3). Technical Report, Microsoft Corporation, 2014.

35.   D. Atkins, W. Stallings, P. Zimmerman, PGP Message Exchange Formats, IETF RFC1991, August 1996, Internet Engineering Task Force.

36.   C. Ellison et. al, SPKI Certificate Theory, IETF RFC2693, September 1999. Internet Engineering Task Force.

37.   C. Adams and S. Farrell, "Internet X.509 Public Key Infrastructure Certificate Management Protocols," RFC 2510, IETF, Mar. 1999, obsoleted by *RFC 4210*.

REFERENCES | CHAPTER 3

1. A. Pentland, D. Shrier, T. Hardjono, and I. Wladawsky-Berger, Towards an Internet of Trusted Data: A New Framework for Identity and Data Sharing: Input to the Whitehouse Commission on Enhancing National Cybersecurity. MIT Connection Science. August 2016.

2. Y. A. de Montjoye and A. Pentland, The MIT OPAL Project, 2015, http://opalproject.org.

3. G. Zyskind, G., O. Nathan, and A. Pentland. Decentralizing privacy: Using blockchain to protect personal data. In Proceedings of 2015 IEEE Symposium on Security and Privacy Workshops, 180-184.

4. A. Pentland, "Reality Mining of Mobile Communications: Toward a New Deal on Data," in The Global Information Technology Report 2008-2009: Mobility in a Networked World, S. Dutta and I. Mia, Eds. World Economic Forum, 2009, pp. 75–80, available on http://hd.media.mit.edu/wef_globalit.pdf.

5. Y. A. de Montjoye, S. S. Wang, and A. Pentland, "On the trusted use of large-scale personal data," IEEE Data Eng. Bull., vol. 35, no. 4, pp. 5–8, 2012.

6. Y. A. de Montjoye, E. Shmueli, S. Wang, and A. Pentland, "openPDS: Regaining ownership and privacy of personal data," 2013.

7. A. Pentland, T. Reid, and T. Heibeck, Big data and Health - Revolutionizing medicine and Public Health: Report of the Big Data and Health Working Group 2013, World Innovation Summit for Health, Qatar Foundation. http://www.wish-qatar.org/app/media/382.

8. Alex Pentland, David Lazer, Devon Brewer, and Tracy Heibeck, "Using Reality Mining to Improve Public Health and Medicine," Studies in Health Technology and Informatics 149 (2009): 93– 102.

9. Y. A. de Montjoye, J. Quoidbach, F. Robic, and A. Pentland, "Predicting personality using novel mobile phone-based metrics," in Social Computing, Behavioral-Cultural Modeling and Prediction (LCNS Vol. 7812). Springer, 2013, pp. 48–55.

10. D. Chaum, C. Crepeau & I. Damgard. "Multiparty unconditionally secure protocols". STOC 1987.

11. S. Goldwasser and S. Micali. Probabilistic encryption and how to play mental poker keeping secret all partial information. In Proceedings of the 14th ACM Symposium on Theory of Computing (STOC'82), pages 365–377, San Francisco, CA, USA, May 1982.

12. A. Yao, "Protocols for secure computations". FOCS. 23rd Annual Symposium on Foundations of Computer Science (FOCS 1982): 160–164

13. A. Shamir, "How to share a secret", Communications of the ACM, 22 (11): 612–613. ACM 1979.

REFERENCES | CHAPTER 4

1. Jonathan Woetzel et al., "Preparing for China's Urban Billion" (McKinsey Global Institute, March 2009), http:// www.mckinsey.com/ insights/ urbanization/ preparing_for_urban_billion_in_china .

2. David Lazer, Alex Sandy Pentland, Lada Adamic, Sinan Aral, Albert Laszlo Barabasi, Devon Brewer, Nicholas Christakis, Noshir Contractor, James Fowler, and Myron Gutmann, "Life in the Network: The Coming Age of Computational Social Science," Science 323 (2009): 721– 723.

3. Sinan Aral and Dylan Walker, "Identifying Influential And Susceptible Members Of Social Networks," Science 337 (2012): 337– 341; Alan Mislove, Sune Lehmann, Yong-Yeol Ahn, Jukka-Pekka Onnela, and J. Niels Rosenquist, Pulse of the Nation: U.S. Mood throughout the Day Inferred from Twitter (website), http:// www.ccs. neu.edu/ home/ amislove/ twittermood/ (accessed November 22, 2013); Jessica Vitak, Paul Zube, Andrew Smock, Caleb T. Carr, Nicole Ellison, and Cliff Lampe, "It's Complicated: Facebook Users ' Political Participation in the 2008 Election," Cyberpsychology, Behavior, and Social Networking 14 (2011): 107– 114.

4. Alexis Madrigal, "Dark Social: We Have the Whole History of the Web Wrong," The Atlantic, October 12, 2013, http:// www.theatlantic.com/ technology/ archive/ 2012/ 10/ dark-social-we-have-the-whole-history-of-the-web-wrong/ 263523/ .

5. Nathan Eagle and Alex Pentland, " Reality Mining: Sensing Complex Social Systems," Personal and Ubiquitous Computing 10 (2006): 255– 268; Alex Pentland, "Reality Mining of Mobile Communications: Toward a New Deal on Data," The Global Information Technology Report 2008– 2009 (Geneva: World Economic Forum, 2009), 75– 80.

6. Alex Pentland, David Lazer, Devon Brewer, and Tracy Heibeck, "Using Reality Mining to Improve Public Health and Medicine," Studies in Health Technology and Informatics 149 (2009): 93– 102.

7. Vivek K. Singh, Laura Freeman, Bruno Lepri, and Alex Sandy Pentland, "Classifying Spending Behavior using Socio-Mobile Data," HUMAN 2 (2013): 99– 111.

8. Wei Pan, Yaniv Altshuler, and Alex Sandy Pentland, "Decoding Social Influence and the Wisdom of the Crowd in Financial Trading Network," in 2012 International Conference on Privacy, Security, Risk and Trust (PASSAT), and 2012 International Conference on Social Computing (SocialCom), 203– 209.

9. Kate Greene, "Reality Mining," MIT Technology Review, March/ April 2008, http:// pubs.media.mit.edu/ pubs/ papers/ tr10pdfdownload.pdf .

10. Meglena Kuneva, European Consumer Commissioner, "Keynote Speech," in Roundtable on Online Data Collection, Targeting and Profiling, March 31, 2009, http:// europa.eu/ rapid/ press-release_SPEECH-09-156_en.htm .

11. Kim Gittleson, "How Big Data Is Changing The Cost Of Insurance," BBC News, November 14, 2013, http:// www.bbc.co.uk/ news/ business-24941415 .

12. Aniko Hannak, Piotr Sapiezynski, Kakhki Arash Molavi, Balachander Krishnamurthy, David Lazer, Alan Mislove, and Christo Wilson, "Measuring Personalization of Web Search," in Proc. 22nd International Conference on World Wide Web (WWW 2013), 527– 538.

13. Pentland, "Reality Mining of Mobile Communications."

14. Anmol Madan, Manuel Cebrian, David Lazer, and Alex Pentland, "Social Sensing for Epidemiological Behavior Change," in Proc. 12th ACM International Conference on Ubiquitous Computing (Ubicomp 2010), 291– 300; Pentland et al. "Using Reality Mining to Improve Public Health and Medicine."

15. Wei Pan, Gourab Ghoshal, Coco Krumme, Manuel Cebrian, and Alex Pentland, "Urban Characteristics Attributable to Density-Driven Tie Formation," Nature Communications 4 (2013): article 1961.

16. Lev Grossman, "Iran Protests: Twitter, the Medium of the Movement," Time Magazine, June 17, 2009; Ellen Barry, "Protests in Moldova Explode, with Help of Twitter," The New York Times, April 8, 2009.

17. "Directive 95/ 46/ EC of the European Parliament and of the Council of 24 October 1995 on the Protection of Individuals with Regard to the Processing of Personal Data and on the Free Movement of Such Data," Official Journal L281 (November 23, 1995): 31– 50.

18. World Economic Forum, "Personal Data: The Emergence of a New Asset Class," January 2011, http:// www.weforum.org/ reports/ personal-data-emergence-new-asset-class .

19. Ibid.

20. Ibid.

21. Antonio Lima, Manlio De Domenico, Veljko Pejovic, and Mirco Musolesi, "Exploiting Cellular Data for Disease Containment and Information Campaign Strategies in Country-Wide Epidemics," School of Computer Science Technical Report CSR-13-01, University of Birmingham, May 2013.

22. Arvind Narayanan and Vitaly Shmatikov, "Robust De-Anonymization of Large Sparse Datasets," in Proc. 2008 IEEE Symposium on Security and Privacy (SP), 111– 125.

23. Latanya Sweeney, "Simple Demographics Often Identify People Uniquely," Data

Privacy Working Paper 3, Carnegie Mellon University, Pittsburgh, 2000.

24. de Montjoye, Yves-Alexandre, Samuel S. Wang, Alex Pentland, "On the Trusted Use of Large-Scale Personal Data," IEEE Data Engineering Bulletin 35, no. 4 (2012): 5– 8.

25. Chaoming Song, Zehui Qu, Nicholas Blumm, and Albert-Laszlo Barabasi, "Limits of Predictability in Human Mobility," Science 327 (2010): 1018– 1021.

26. Pentland et al., "Using Reality Mining to Improve Public Health and Medicine."

27. David Tacconi, Oscar Mayora, Paul Lukowicz, Bert Arnrich, Cornelia Setz, Gerhard Troster, and Christian Haring, "Activity and Emotion Recognition to Support Early Diagnosis of Psychiatric Diseases," in Proc. 2nd International ICST Conference on Pervasive Computing Technologies for Healthcare, 100– 102.

28. World Economic Forum, "Personal Data."

29. The White House, "National Strategy for Trusted Identities in Cyberspace: Enhancing Online Choice, Efficiency, Security, and Privacy," Washington, DC, April 2011, http:// www.whitehouse.gov/ sites/ default/ files/ rss_viewer/ NSTICstrategy_041511. pdf .

30. Thomas Hardjono, "User-Managed Access UMA Profile of OAuth2.0 ," Internet draft, 2013, http:// docs.kantarainitiative.org/ uma/ draft-uma-core.html.

31. A Creative Commons licensed example set of integrated business and technical system rules for the institutional use of personal data stores is available athttps://github.com/HumanDynamics/SystemRules.

32. See http:// openPDS.media.mit.edu for project information and https://github. com/HumanDynamics/openPDS for the open source code.

33. Nick Bilton, "Girls around Me: An App Takes Creepy to a New Level," The New York Times, Bits (blog), March 30, 2012, http:// bits.blogs.nytimes.com/2012/03/30/ girls-around-me-ios-app-takes-creepy-to-a-new-level .

34. U.S. Environmental Protection Agency, RCRA Corrective Action Program, "Institutional Controls Glossary," Washington, DC, 2007,http://www.epa.gov/ epawaste/hazard/correctiveaction/resources/guidance/ics/glossary1.pdf .

35. University of Florida , Center for Environmental & Human Toxicology, "Development of Cleanup Target Levels (CTLs) for Chapter 62-777, F.A.C.," Technical report, Florida Department of Environmental Protection, Division of Waste Management, February 2005, http:// www.dep.state.fl.us/ waste/ quick_topics/ publications/ wc/ FinalGuidanceDocumentsFlowCharts_April2005/ TechnicalReport2FinalFeb2005 (Final3-28-05). pdf.

36. U.S. Environmental Protection Agency, "Institutional Controls: A Guide to Planning, Implementing, Maintaining, and Enforcing Institutional Controls at

Contaminated Sites," OSWER 9355.0-89, Washington, DC, December 2012, http:// www.epa.gov/ superfund/ policy/ ic/ guide/ Final% 20PIME% 20Guidance% 20December% 202012. pdf .

37. Ralph A . DeMeo and Sarah Meyer Doar, "Restrictive Covenants as Institutional Controls for Remediated Sites: Worth the Effort?" The Florida Bar Journal 85, no. 2 (February 2011); Florida Department of Environmental Protection, Division of Waste Management, "Institutional Controls Procedures Guidance," Tallahassee, June 2012, http:// www.dep.state.fl.us/ waste/ quick_topics/ publications/ wc/ csf/ icpg.pdf ; University of Florida, "Development of Cleanup Target Levels."

38. World Economic Forum, "Personal Data."

39. Thomas Hardjono, Daniel Greenwood, and Alex Pentland, "Towards a Trustworthy Digital Infrastructure for Core Identities and Personal Data Stores," in Proc. ID360 Conference on Identity, University of Texas, Austin. 2013.

40. Thomas Hardjono and Eve Maler, "User-Managed Access UMA Profile of OAuth2.0,"Binding Obligations on User-Managed Access (UMA) Participants," Internet Draft, 2013, http:// docs.kantarainitiative.org/ uma/ draft-uma-trust. html

41. Simon Barber, Xavier Boyen, Elaine Shi, and Ersin Uzun, "Bitter to Better – How to Make Bitcoin a Better Currency," in Proc. Financial Cryptography and Data Security Conference (2012), LNCS 7397, 399– 414.

42. Stan Stalnaker, "About [Ven Currency]," http:// www.ven.vc (accessed January 16, 2014).

43. Thomas Hardjono , Patrick Deegan, and John Clippinger, "On the Design of Trustworthy Compute Frameworks for Self-Organizing Digital Institutions," in Proc. 16th International Conference on Human-Computer Interaction, HCI (2014)."

44. See e.g. the study SensibleDTU (https:// www.sensible.dtu.dk/? lang = en). This study of 1,000 freshman students at the Technical University of Denmark gives students mobile phones in order to study their networks and social behavior during an important change in their lives. It uses not only data collected from the mobile phones (such as location, Bluetooth-based proximity, and call and sms logs), but also from social networks and questionnaires filled out by participants.

Attribution:

This material has been published as Chapter 9 in the book "Privacy, Big Data, and the Public Good" edited by Julia Lane, Victoria

Stodden, Stefan Bender, and Helen Nissenbaum, [and is reproduced by permission of Cambridge University Press]. For more information on this book, please see:

- Cambridge University Press': Books Online: http://dx.doi.org/10.1017/CBO9781107590205 and http://www.cambridge.org/9781107637689 and

- The Amazon.com book page: http://www.amazon.com/Privacy-Big-Data-Public-Good/dp/1107637686

REFERENCES | CHAPTER 5

[1]   Acquisti, A., Brandimarte, L., and Loewenstein, G. Privacy and the human behavior in the age of information. Science, 347(6221), (2015), 509-514.

[2]   Adar, E., and Huberman, B. A market for secrets. First Monday, 6(8), (2001).

[3]   Benkler, Y. The Wealth of Networks. Yale University Press, New Haven, CT, 2006.

[4]   Carrascal, J.P., Riederer, C., Erramilli, V., Cherubini, M., and de Oliveira, R. Your browsing behavior for a big mac: Economics of personal information online. In Proceedings of the 22nd International Conference on World Wide Web (Rio de Janeiro, Brazil, May 13-17). ACM Press, New York, 2013, 189-200.

[5]   Centellegher, S., De Nadai, M., Caraviello, M., Leonardi, C., Vescovi, M., Ramadian, Y., Oliver, N., Pianesi, F., Pentland, A., Antonelli, F., and Lepri, B. The Mobile Territorial Lab: A multilayered and dynamic view on parents' daily lives. EPJ Data Science, in press.

[6]   Cvrcek, D., Kumpost, M., Matyas, V., and Danezis, G. A study on the value of the location privacy. In Proceedings of the 5th ACM workshop on Privacy in Electronic Society (Alexandria, VA, USA, October 30). ACM Press, New York, 2006, 109-118.

[6]   Danezis, G., Lewis, S., and Anderson R.J. How much is location privacy worth? In Proceedings of 4th Workshop on the Economics of Information Security (Cambridge, MA, USA, June 2-3). 2005.

[7]   De Filippi, P. The interplay between decentralization and privacy: The case of blockchain technologies. Journal of Peer Production, 7, (2015).

[8]   Lathia, N., Pejovic, V., Rachuri, K. Mascolo, C., Musolesi, M., and Rentfrow, P.J. Smartphones for large-scale behavior change interventions. IEEE Pervasive Computing, 12(3), (2014), 2-9.

[9]   Lazer, D., Pentland, A., Adamic, L., Aral, S., Barabasi, A.-L., Brewer, D., Christakis, N., Contractor, N., Fowler, J., Gutmann, M., Jebara, T., King G., Macy, M, Roy D., and Van Alstyne, M. Computational social science, Science, 323(5915), (2009), 721.

[10] Mun, M., Hao, S., Mishra, N., Shilton, K., Burke, J., Estrin, D., Hansen, M., and Govindan, R. Personal data vaults: A locus of control for personal data streams. In Proceedings of the 6th ACM International COnference, Co-NEXT'10 (Philadelphia, PA, USA, November 30 – December 3). ACM Press, New York, 2010, 1-12.

[11] de Montjoye, Y.-A., Hidalgo, C., Verleysen, M., and Blondel, V. Unique in the crowd: The privacy bounds of human mobility. Scientific Reports, 3, (2013).

[12] de Montjoye, Y.-A., Shmueli, E., Wang, S., and Pentland, A. OpenPDS: Protecting the privacy of metadata through SafeAnswers. PloS One, 10.1371, (2014).

13 Nakamoto, S. Bitcoin: A peer-to-peer electronic cash system, cs.kent.edu, (2009).

14 Pentland, A. Society's nervous system: Building effective government, energy, and public health systems. IEEE Computer, 45(1), (2012), 31-38.

15 Pentland, A. Reality mining of mobile communications: Toward a new deal on data. World Economic Forum Global IT Report 2008, Chapter 1.6, (2008), 75-80

16 Rainie, L., and Duggan, M. Privacy and information sharing. Pew Research Center, http://www.pewinternet.org/2016/01/14/privacy-and-information-sharing/ (2016).

17 Schneier, B. Data and Goliath: The hidden battles to collect your data and to control your world. Norton and Company, New York City, NY, USA, 2015.

18 Shamir, A. How to share a secret. Communications of the ACM, 22(11), (1979), 612-613.

19 Staiano, J., Oliver, N., Lepri, B., de Oliveira, R., Caraviello, M. and Sebe, N. Money walks: a human-centric study on the economics of personal mobile data. In Proceedings of the 2014 ACM International Joint Conference on Pervasive and Ubiquitous Computing (Seattle, WA, USA, September 13-17). ACM Press, New York, (2014), 583-594.

20 Szabo, N. Formalizing and securing relationships on public networks. First Monday, 2(9), (1997).

21 Tsai, J., Kelley, P. Cranor, L., and Sadeh, N. Location sharing technologies: Privacy risks and controls. I/S: A Journal of Law and Policy for the Information Society, 6(2), (2010), 119-151.

22 Urban, J.M., Hoofnagle, C.J., and Li, S. Mobile phones and privacy. BLCT Research Paper Series. (July 11, 2012).

23 Want, R., Pering, T., Danneels, G., Kumar, M., Sundar, M., and Light, J. (2002). The personal server: Changing the way we think about ubiquitous computing. In Proceedings of 4th International Conference on Ubiquitous Computing (Goteborg, Sweden, September 29 – October 1), ACM Press, New York, (2002), 194-209.

24 Zyskind, G., Nathan, O., and Pentland, A. (2015). Decentralizing privacy: Using blockchain to protect personal data. In Proceedings of IEEE Symposium on Security and Privacy Workshops, 180-184.

25 http://www.orange.com/en/content/download/21358/412063/version/5/file/ Orange+Future+of+Digital+Trust+Report.pdf

26 Zyskind, Guy, Oz Nathan, and Alex Pentland. "Enigma: Decentralized computation platform with guaranteed privacy." arXiv preprint arXiv:1506.03471 (2015).

REFERENCES | CHAPTER 6

[1]   ITU, (2013) ICT Facts and Figures http://www.itu.int/en/ITU-D/Statistics/
Documents/facts/ICTFacts- Figures2013-e.pdf.

[2]   For a longer piece on the various ways in which mobile data can be used
in the development sphere see: Kendall et al. (2014) Using Mobile Data for
Development http://www.impatientoptimists.org/ Posts/2014/07/Big-Data-and-
How-it-Can-Serve-Development.

[3]   Wesolowski, A., Eagle, N., Tatem, A. J., Smith, D. L., Noor, A. M., Snow, R.
W., and Buckee, C. O. (2012). Quan- tifying the impact of human mobility
on malaria. Science, 338(6104), 267-270. http://www.sciencemag.org/con-
tent/338/6104/267.abstract.

[4]   Examples include: WorldPop (2014) Ebola http://www.worldpop.org.uk/ebola/;
Eagle, N., Macy, M., and Claxton, R. (2010). Network diversity and economic
development. Science, 328 (5981), 1029-1031. http://www.sciencemag.org/
content/328/5981/1029; or Eagle, N., de Montjoye, Y., and Bettencourt, L. M.
(2009). Community computing: Com- parisons between rural and urban societies
using mobile phone data. In IEEE Computational Science and Engineer- ing, 2009.
http://doi.ieeecomputersociety.org/10.1109/CSE.2009.91.

[5]   Wesolowski, A., Buckee, C. O., Bengtsson, L., Wetter, E., Lu, X., and Tatem, A. J.
(2014). Commentary: Containing the Ebola Outbreak–the Potential and Challenge
of Mobile Network Data. PLOS Currents Outbreaks.

[6]   Call for Help & Waiting on Hold, The Economist, Oct. 25, 2014.

[7]   Sundsøy, P., Bjelland, J., Iqbal, A., Pentland, A., and de Montjoye, Y. A. (2014).
Big Data-Driven Marketing: How Ma- chine Learning Outperforms Marketers'
Gut-Feeling. In Social Computing, Behavioral-Cultural Modeling and Predic- tion,
367-374.

[8]   This is very similar to how some mobile marketing interfaces work where
marketers will specify the criteria and identifying characteristics for the people
they want to target with specific messages but would not receive actual numbers.
Alternatively, anonymized data could be shared with encrypted identifiers which
would be passed back to the operator to trigger outreach.

[9]   One example is the open Data for Development contest run by Orange, de
Montjoye, Y. A., Smoreda, Z., Trin- quart, R., Ziemlicki, C., and Blondel, V. D. (2014).
D4D-Senegal: The Second Mobile Phone Data for Development Challenge. arXiv
preprint arXiv:1407.4885. http://arxiv.org/abs/1407.4885.

[10] U.N. Global Pulse (2014) Data Philanthropy: Where Are We Now?, http://www.

unglobalpulse.org/data-philanthro- py-where-are-we-now.

[11] 45 C.F.R. 164.514.

[12] de Montjoye, Y. A., Hidalgo, C. A., Verleysen, M., and Blondel, V. D. (2013). Unique in the Crowd: The privacy bounds of human mobility. Nature SRep, 3. http://www.nature.com/srep/2013/130325/srep01376/full/srep01376.html.

[13] Executive Office of The President, Office of Management & Budget, Safeguarding Against And Responding to The Loss of Personal Information, Memorandum M-07-16 (May 22, 2007).

[14] European Union, Directive 95/46/EC, Recital 26.

[15] Article 29 Data Protection Working Party, Opinion 05/2014 on Anonymisation Techniques. 0829/14/EN (April 10, 2014).

[16] Bengtsson, L., Lu, X., Thorson, A., Garfield, R., and Von Schreeb, J. (2011). Improved response to disasters and outbreaks by tracking population movements with mobile phone network data: a post-earthquake geospatial study in Haiti. PLoS medicine, 8(8), e1001083.

[17] The back-of-the envelope reasoning goes as: We use a spatial resolution of 17 antennas on average ($v = 17$) and a temporal resolution of 12 hours ($h = 12$). This means that with 4 points in a given month, we'd have a ~20% chance ($\mathcal{E} = .20$) at re-identifying an individual in a given month (resp. $\mathcal{E} = .55$ with 10 points)(see http://www.nature.com/srep/2013/130325/srep01376/fig_tab/srep01376_F4.html). This means that, to have between 20% to 55% chances of re-identifying an individual, we'd need 4 to 10 points every month meaning 48 to 120 points total for a year. Even in this case, as we use a 5% sampling and we resample every month, an individual has only a 45% chance to be in at least one of the sampled month ($1 - 0.95 \wedge 12$ months).

[18] Bandicoot, a python toolbox to extract behavioral indicators from metadata http://bandicoot.mit.edu/.

[19] For a discussion of the use of mobile data to direct aid delivery in the 2010 Haiti earthquake see Bengtsson, L., Lu, X., Thorson, A., Garfield, R., and Von Schreeb, J. (2011).

[20] We assume here that the mobile operator does not have explicit permission from the data subject to disclose their information. If users were to opt-in to sharing this would then become permissible.

[21] https://github.com/yvesalexandre/privacy-tools/.

[22] de Montjoye, Y. A., Shmueli, E., Wang, S. S., and Pentland, A. S. (2014). openPDS: Protecting the Pri- vacy of Metadata through SafeAnswers. PloS One, 9(7), e98790. http://www.plosone.org/article/

info%3Adoi%2F10.1371%2Fjournal.pone.0098790; and de Montjoye, Y. A., Wang, S. S., Pentland, A. (2012). On the Trusted Use of Large-Scale Personal Data. IEEE Data Eng. Bull., 35(4), 5-8.

23   While promising, these solutions are not yet ready for prime-time. Standardized software to process call detail records along with testing and reporting tools are still under development while the use of online systems allowing researchers to ask questions that would be run against the data and only receive answers would imply architectures investments from mobile phone operators.

24   IMEI or International Mobile Station Equipment, a unique number that identifies a mobile phone on the network.

25   One potentially interesting solution here would be to rely on multiple hash functions that can be nested.

26   BBC News, Ebola: Can big data analytics help contain its spread? http://www.bbc.com/news/business-29617831.

27   European Union, Directive 95/46/EC, Article 7 (d), (e). An update to this legislation, the Privacy Regulation proposed by the European Commission in 2012, http://ec.europa.eu/justice/data-protection/document/review2012/ com_2012_11_en.pdf, also included an exception from certain requirements for "scientific, historical, statistical, and scientific research purposes,' but this was removed from legislation as passed by the European Parliament. http:// www.europarl.europa.eu/meetdocs/2009_2014/documents/libe/pr/922/922387/922387en.pdf.

28   Under the World Health Organization's International Health Regulations, the WHO and member states under- take to conduct "surveillance" for public health purposes and member states are permitted to "disclose and process personal data where essential for purposes of assessing and managing public health risks." WHO, Fifty-eighth World Health Assembly Resolution WHA58.3: Revision of the International Health Regulations, Articles 1 (definition of surveillance), 5.4, and 45 . 2005, http://www.who.int/ipcs/publications/wha/ihr_resolution.pdf.

29   No silver bullet: De-identification still doesn't work https://freedom-to-tinker.com/blog/randomwalker/no-silver- bullet-de-identification-still-doesnt-work/.

30   Draft African Union Convention On The Establishment Of A Credible Legal Framework For Cyber Security In Africa http://www.au.int/en/cyberlegislation.

REFERENCES | CHAPTER 7

[1]   Mani A, Michelle-Loock C, Rahwan I, Staake T, Fliesch E, Pentland A, (2013) "Incentives Promote Peer Pressure in an Energy Saving Campaign," in submission (presented at Netsci, 2013 and Behavior Energy and Climate Change Conference, 2013).

[2]   World Bank 2015 Global Findex

REFERENCES | APPENDIX A

[1]   Many of these concepts and background information have been introduced in: Davis, Marc, Ron Martinez and Chris Kalaboukis. "Rethinking Personal Information – Workshop Pre-read." Invention Arts and World Economic Forum, June 2010.

[2]   Bain & Company Industry Brief. "Using Data as a Hidden Asset." August 16, 2010.

[3]   Angwin, Julia. "The Web's New Gold Mine: Your Secrets." Wall Street Journal. July 30, 2010. http://online. wsj.com/article/SB10001424052748703940904575395073512989404.html

[4]   IDC. "The Digital Universe Decade – Are You Ready?" May 2010.

[5]   The Economist. "Data, Data Everywhere." February 25, 2010.

[6]   The Radicati Group. "Email Statistics Report, 2009–2013." May 2009.

[7]   "Twitter + Ping = Discovering More Music." Twitter Blog. November 11, 2010; "Statistics." Facebook Press Room. January 11, 2011. http://www.facebook.com/press/info.php?statistics

[8]   Nokia Siemens Networks. "Digital Safety, Putting Trust into the Customer Experience." Unite Magazine. Issue 7. http://www.nokiasiemensnetworks.com/news-events/publications/unite-magazine-february-2010/ digital-safety-putting-trust-into-the-customer

[9]   Javelin Strategy & Research. "The 2010 Identity Fraud Survey Report." February 10, 2010.

[10]   David, Scott. K&L Gates and Open Identity Exchange ABA Document. October 20, 2010

[11]   In the US, recent developments emerging from the NSTIC, the Federal Trade Commission and the Department of Commerce warrant attention. In the EU, companies should work with the European Commission's efforts to revise the EU privacy directive and to synchronise legislation across its member states.

[12]   Ericsson [press release]. "CEO to Shareholders: 50 Billion Connections 2020." April 13, 2010.

[13]   Cisco. "Cisco Visual Networking Index: Global Mobile Data; Traffic Forecast Update, 2009 – 2014." February 9, 2010.

[14]   IDC. "The Digital Universe Decade – Are You Ready?" May 2010.

[15]   Definition based on Directive 95/46/EC of the European Parliament and the Council of 24, October 1995.

[16]   Davis, Marc, Ron Martinez and Chris Kalaboukis. "Rethinking Personal Information – Workshop Pre-read." Invention Arts and World Economic Forum,

[33] See, for example, Cate, Fred H. "The Failure of Fair Information Practice Principles." Consumer Protection in the Age of the Information Economy, 2006.

[17] Ibid.

[18] "Fair Information Practice Principles (FIPP)." Federal Trade Commission (FTC). 1998. Discussion

[34] As If Deal, Wynn. "Revised EU Privacy Advisory Board Greater Than US Legal Policy on the Web." Computerworld.com., November 5, 2010.

[35] Strauser, Kirk. "The History and Future of SMTP." FSM, March 4, 2005.

[36] In 2000, the US Safe Harbor Framework was agreed that would allow US organizations to abide by the EU's privacy directive serving the developing need for cross-border data flow. See Mizelle W., Peder W. agreement.

[37] See Davis, Mass, Rond et al. Privacy Rights Federal Trade Commission. "US/EU Safe Harbor Agreement: What It Is and What It Says About the Future." World Economic Forum. June 2010. harbor.pdf

[38] Clippinger, John. Berkman Center for Internet & Society at Harvard University.

[39] To learn more about how companies are using new and intrusive Internet-tracking technologies, see "What They Know" (series). Wall Street Journal. 2010. http://online.wsj.com/public/page/what-they-know- digital-privacy.html

[23] National Strategy for Trusted Identities in Cyberspace. Draft. June 25, 2010.

[24] Reed, Drummond. "Person Data Ecosystem." Podcast Episode 2, December 2010.

[25] "National Strategy for Trusted Identities." Draft pages 8–9. June 25, 2010.

[26] 'Blue Button' Provides Access to Downloadable Personal Health Data." Office of Science and Technology Policy, the White House website. http://www. whitehouse.gov/blog/2010/10/07/blue-button-provides-access- downloadable-personal-health-data

[27] CyberSource. 11th Annual "Online Fraud Report." 2010.

[28] 2009 "Internet Crime Report." Internet Crime Complaint Center. US Department of Justice, 2010

[29] Higgins Open Source Identity Framework is a project of The Eclipse Foundation. Ottawa, Ontario, Canada. http://www.eclipse.org/higgins/faq.php.

[30] Kreizman, Gregg, Ray Wagner and Earl Perkins. "Open Identity Pilot Advances the Maturity of User-Cen- tric Identity, but Business Models Are Still Needed." Gartner, November 9, 2009. http://www.gartner.com/ DisplayDocument?id=1223830

[31] Cybersource. "11th Annual Online Fraud Report." 2010.

[32] See, for example, Connolly, Chris. "The US Safe Harbor – Fact or Fiction?" Galexia,

REFERENCES | APPENDIX B

[i] See, e.g., http://www-01.ibm.com/software/data/ bigdata/what-is-big-data.html

[ii] ECLAC (2014). "Latin American Economic Outlook 2013: SME Policies for Structural Change", p. 124 (http://www.cepal.org/publicaciones/xml/5/48385/leo2013_ing.pdf)

[iii] McKinsey Global Institute (November 2013). "Lions go digital: The Internet's transformative potential in Africa." (http://www.mckinsey.com/insights/high_tech_telecoms_internet/lions_go_digital_the_ internets_transformative_potential_in_africa)

[iv] See Ugandan Ministry of Health (www.mtrac.ug)

[v] Enns, E.A and Amuasi, J.H. (2013). "Human mobility and communication patterns in Côte d'Ivoire: A network perspective for malaria control", published in Mobile Phone Data for Development: Analysis of mobile phone datasets for the development of Ivory Coast. Selected Contributions to the D4D challenge sponsored by Orange. (http://perso.uclouvain.be/ vincent.blondel/netmob/2013/D4D-book.pdf)

[vi] The coding of the nature of the data in the MDG database (http://mdgs.un.org/unsd/mdg/Data.aspx) is as follows:Country data: Produced and disseminated by the country (including data adjusted by the country to meet international standards).

· Country data adjusted: Produced and provided by the country, but adjusted by the international agency for international comparability to comply with internationally agreed standards, definitions and classifications.

· Estimated: Estimated are based on national data, such as surveys or administrative records, or other sources but on the same variable being estimated, produced by the international agency when country data for some year(s) is not available, when multiple sources exist, or when there are data quality issues.

· Modelled: Modelled by the agency on the basis of other covariates when there is a complete lack of data on the variable being estimated.

· Global monitoring data: Produced on a regular basis by the designated agency for global monitoring, based on country data. There is no corresponding figure at the country level.

[vii] UNICEF (2013). Every Child's Birth Right: Inequities and trends in birth registration. (http://www.unicef.org/ mena/MENA-Birth_Registration_report_low_res-01.pdf)

viii   A UN Women's compilation of country surveys on violence against Woman is available from http://www.endvawnow.org/uploads/browser/files/vawprevalence_matrix_june2013.pdf

ix   UNHCR (June 2014). "UNHCR Global Trends 2013: War's Human Cost". (http://unhcr.org/trends2013/)

x   This is also the aim of the initiatives launched around the world to go 'Beyond GDP'. For a review of these initiatives see www.wikiprogress.org

xi   UN Global Pulse (June 2013). Big Data for Development: A Primer, p.4 (http://www.unglobalpulse.org/bigdataprimer)

xii   UK Department for Business, Innovation & Skills and Cabinet Office (May 2013). "Market assessment of public sector information." (https://www.gov.uk/government/publications/ public-sector-information-market-assessment)

xiii   Chui, M. Farrell, D. and Jackson, K. (April 2014). "How government can promote open data". McKinsey&Company. (http://www.mckinsey.com/insights/public_sector/ how_government_can_promote_open_data)

xiv   Kumar, R. (2014) "How Youth Saved Bananas in Uganda" (http://blogs.worldbank.org/youthink/ how-youth-saved-bananas-uganda)

xv   Pentland, A. (October 2013). "The Data Driven Society", Scientific American, pp. 78-83

xvi   World Bank and WHO (May 2014). Global Civil Registration and Vital Statistics Scaling Up Investment Plan 2015-2024. Working Paper 88351. (http://www.worldbank.org/en/topic/health/publication/ global-civil-registration-vital-statistics-scaling-up- investment)

xvii   The World Bank Group and the governments of Canada, Norway, and the United States

CONTRIBUTOR BIOGRAPHIES

CONTRIBUTOR BIOGRAPHIES

Thomas Hardjono is the CTO of MIT Connection Science and Engineering. He leads technical projects and initiatives around identity, security and data privacy, and engages industry partners and sponsors on these fronts. Thomas is also the technical director for the Internet Trust Consortium under MIT Connection Science that implements open source software based on cutting edge research at MIT. Previous to this Thomas was the Director of the MIT Kerberos Consortium, developing the famous MIT Kerberos authentication software currently used by millions of users around the world. He has been active in the areas of security, applied cryptography and identity management for nearly two decades now, starting from the mid-1990s working in the emerging PKI industry as Principal Scientist at VeriSign, which became the largest PKI provider in the world. His work included devices certificates for DOCSIS cable modems, WiFi devices and the Trusted Platform Module (TPM) security hardware. He has chaired a number of key technical groups, including in the IETF, OASIS, Trusted Computing Group, Kantara and other organizations. At MIT Thomas has also been instrumental in the development of the OpenID-Connect 1.0 protocol (OIDC), standing-up the first OIDC service at a major university (oidc.mit.edu). Over the years he has published three books and over sixty technical papers in journals and at conferences. He holds 19 patents in the areas of security and cryptography. Thomas has a BSc degree in Computer Science with Honors from the University of Sydney, and PhD degree in Computer Science from the University of New South Wales in Australia.

David Shrier is Managing Director of MIT Connection Science and leads creation and launch of other new initiatives for the

Massachusetts Institute of Technology. He is also on the advisory board of WorldQuant University, which offers a totally free, online, accredited master's degree in analytics. David recently advised the European Commission on commercializing innovation with a focus on digital technology, and advises private and public companies on corporate innovation. David specializes in building new revenue on established platforms, having developed $8.5 billion of growth opportunities with companies including GE/NBC Universal, Dun & Bradstreet, Wolters Kluwer, Disney, Ernst & Young, AOL Verizon, and Starwood Hotels & Resorts, as well as leading private equity and VC funds. He has also started and/or led a number of private equity and venture capital-backed companies as CEO, CFO or COO. David created a revolutionary online Fintech startup learning experience for MIT called "Fintech Innovation: Future Commerce", that has deployed into 89 countries, and also teaches courses and workshops for MIT such as "Data Academy", "Inspiring Change: Strategic Narrative for Startup Success", "Big Data and Social Analytics", and "Future Health". His first book, together with Sandy Pentland, is *Frontiers of Financial Technology*. David Shrier was granted an Sc.B. from Brown University in Biology and Theatre.

Professor Alex "Sandy" Pentland holds a triple appointment at the Massachusetts Institute of Technology in the Media Lab (SA+P), School of Engineering and School of Management. He also directs MIT's Connect Science initiative, the Human Dynamics Laboratory and the MIT Media Lab Entrepreneurship Program, and has been a member of the Advisory Boards for Google, Nissan, Telefonica, Tencent, and a variety of start-up firms. For several years he co-led the World Economic Forum Big Data and Personal Data initiatives. He has pioneered the fields of wearable computing and computational social science, generating several successful startups and technology spinoffs. Sandy was recently named by the Secretary-General of the United Nations to the Independent Expert Advisory Group on the Data Revolution for Sustainable Development. His article, "The New Science of Building Great Teams", won paper of the year in 2012 from Harvard Business Review. Sandy has previously helped create and direct MIT's Media Laboratory, the Media Lab Asia laboratories at the Indian Institutes of Technology, and Strong Hospital's Center for Future Health. He recently led a task force on big data & healthcare for the World Innovation Summit in Healthcare, held in Doha, Qatar. In 2012 Forbes named Sandy one of the "seven most powerful data scientists in the world", along with the founders of Google and the CTO of the United States, and in 2013 he won the McKinsey Award from Harvard Business Review. Prof. Pentland's books include *Honest Signals, Social Physics*, and *Frontiers of Financial Technology.* He was named to the National Academy of Engineering in 2014. Sandy holds a BGS from the University of Michigan and a Ph.D. from MIT.

Daniel "Dazza" Greenwood is an entrepreneur, innovator and national thought on design and deployment of scalable, distributed Trust Network and other digital systems. Dazza heads the digital business systems design and architecture firm CIVICS.com, which he founded in 1996. At MIT Media Lab and MIT Connection Science, Dazza lecturers and conducts R&D on big data, digital identity federation, personal data sharing and is developing the field of computational law and jurimetrics through law.MIT.edu events and projects. Privately, Dazza provides professional consultancy services to industry, government and civic organizations, including fortune 50 companies, national governments, and marketplaces through CIVICS.com. Dazza has catalyzed or led numerous industry, governmental and public-private initiatives aimed at developing innovative legal solutions, technical standards and business models.

Jake Kendall is the Director of the Digital Financial Services Innovation Lab (DFS Lab) housed at Caribou Digital. Formerly Jake was Deputy Director of Research and Emerging Technologies within the Financial Services for the Poor Team at the Gates Foundation where his team helped create the global data architecture for tracking financial inclusion and invested to create high potential emerging technologies. Jake is a published researcher and author and holds a PhD in Economics from UC Santa Cruz and a BS in Physics from MIT. Prior to joining the Gates foundation, he spent time as an Economist with the Consultative Group to Assist the Poor (CGAP) within the World Bank and in two fintech start-ups in the field of public key cryptography. Jake also spent two years in Zambia as a fisheries extension agent with the US Peace Corps and worked, throughout his youth, a salmon fisherman in Alaska.

Cameron Kerry is a Visiting Scholar at the MIT Media Lab, a Distinguished Visiting Fellow at the Brookings Institution, and Senior Counsel at Sidley Austin, LLP in Boston and Washington, DC. His practice at Sidley Austin involves privacy, security, and international trade issues. Kerry served as General Counsel and Acting Secretary of the United States Department of Commerce, where he was a leader on a wide of range of issues laying a new foundation for U.S. economic growth in a global marketplace. He continues to speak and write on these issues, particularly privacy and data security, intellectual property, and international trade. While Acting Secretary, Cameron Kerry served as chief executive of this Cabinet agency and its 43,000 employees around the world, as well as an adviser to the President. His tenure marked the first time in U.S. history two siblings have served in the President's Cabinet at the same time.

Yves-Alexandre de Montjoye is a lecturer at Imperial College London and a research scientist at the MIT Media Lab. He recently received his Ph.D. in computational privacy from MIT. His research aims at understanding how the unicity of human behavior impacts the privacy of individuals--through re-identification or inference--in large-scale metadata datasets such as mobile phone, credit cards, or browsing data. Yves-Alexandre was recently named an Innovator under 35 for Belgium (TR35). His research has been published in Science and Nature SRep. and covered by the BBC, CNN, New York Times, Wall Street Journal, Harvard Business Review, Le Monde, Die Spiegel, Die Zeit, El Pais as well as in his TEDx talks. His work on the shortcomings of anonymization has appeared in reports of the World Economic Forum, United Nations, OECD, FTC, and the European Commission. Before coming to MIT, he was a researcher at the Santa Fe Institute in New Mexico. Yves-Alexandre worked for the Boston Consulting Group and acted as an expert for both the Bill and Melinda Gates Foundation and the United Nations. He is a member of the OECD Advisory Group on Health Data Governance. Over a period of 6 years, he obtained an M.Sc. from Louvain in Applied Mathematics, a M.Sc. (Centralien) from Ecole Centrale Paris, a M.Sc. from KU Leuven in Mathematical Engineering as well as his B.Sc. in engineering at Louvain.

Bruno Lepri leads the Mobile and Social Computing Lab (MobS) and is vice-responsible of the Complex Data Analytics research line at Bruno Kessler Foundation (Trento, Italy). Bruno is also research affiliate at the MIT Media Lab working with the Human Dynamics group and the MIT Connection Science initiative and he recently launched an alliance between MIT and FBK on Human Dynamics Observatories. He is also a senior research affiliate of Data-Pop Alliance, the first think-tank on Big Data and Development co-created by the Harvard Humanitarian Initiative, MIT Media Lab, Overseas Development Institute, and Flowminder to promote a people-centered big data revolution. In 2010 he won a Marie Curie Cofund post-doc fellow and he has held post-doc positions at FBK and at MIT Media Lab. He holds a Ph.D. in Computer Science from the University of Trento. He also serves as consultant of several companies and international organizations. His research interests include computational social science, big data and personal data, pervasive and ubiquitous computing, and human behavior understanding. His research has received attention from several press outlets and obtained the best paper award at ACM Ubicomp 2014.

Nuria Oliver is a computer scientist with a PhD from MIT on perceptual intelligence. She has over 20 years of research experience, first at MIT, then at Microsoft Research (Redmond, WA) and finally as the first female Scientific Director at Telefonica R&D (Barcelona, Spain). Her work on computational human behavior modeling, human-computer interaction, Mobile computing and Big Data analysis, particularly applied for Social Good, is internationally known with over 100 scientific articles in international conferences and journals, cited over 10000 times and with several best paper awards and nominations. She is co-inventor of 40 filed patents and a frequent keynote speaker in international conferences. She is the first Spanish female computer scientist named a Distinguished Scientist by the ACM and a Fellow of the European Association of Artificial Intelligence. Her work has received many international awards, such as the MIT TR100 (today TR35) Young Innovator Award (2004), and the Gaudí Gresol award to Excellence in Science and Technology (2016). She has been selected as one of the "top 9 female technology directors" in Spain by EL PAIS (2012), one of the "100 leaders for the future" by Capital (2009), a Rising Talent by the Women's Forum for the Economy and Society (2009) and one of "40 youngsters with great potential in Spain" by EL PAIS (1999), among others. Her passion is to improve the quality of life of people, both individually and collectively, through technology. She also has great interest for scientific outreach and to inspire new generations –and particularly girls—to pursue careers in technology. Therefore, she is a frequent collaborator with the media and she gives talks both to the general public and especially to thousands of teenagers.

Jacopo Staiano is Research & Data Scientist at Fortia Financial Solutions Lab, and a research affiliate at at the Harvard-ODI-MIT Data-Pop Alliance. Previously, he held post-doctoral positions at LIP6, UPMC - Sorbonne Universités and at the Mobile and Social Computing Lab, Fondazione Bruno Kessler (TN, Italy). He received his B.Eng. degree in Computer Engineering from the University of Pisa, before obtaining a MA in Sonic Arts from the Queen's University of Belfast, and a M.Sc. in Human Language Technology and Interfaces from the University of Trento. He holds a Ph.D. in Information and Communication Technology from the University of Trento. He has been visiting researcher at the Ambient Intelligence Research Lab, Stanford University, the Human Dynamics Lab, MIT Media Lab, and Telefonica I+D. His research interests include Computational Social Science, Affective and Pervasive Computing, Machine Learning and Natural Language Processing. His research has received attention from several press outlets, and obtained the Honorable Mention at

ACM DIS 2012 and the Best Paper Award at ACM UbiComp 2014.

Guy Zyskind is the Founder and CEO of Enigma, a company that enables computing over encrypted data through a mix of secure Multi-party Computation (MPC) and Blockchain technologies. Enigma is the culmination of Guy's graduate thesis at MIT, where he also taught the first blockchain engineering class. Guy has authored several academic papers, most recently on privacy and the blockchain, including the Enigma whitepaper (downloaded over 100K times) and "Decentralizing Privacy: Using Blockchain to Protect Personal Data" that appeared in IEEE SPW 15'. Previously, Guy led the development of several start-up companies. Most notably, he was the Chief Technology Officer at Athena Wisdom (now Endor), an MIT Media Lab spin-off company involving Big Data Analytics and Network Science. Guy holds an M.S. from MIT and a B.S. in Electrical Engineering and Computer Science from Tel-Aviv University.

Made in the USA
Charleston, SC
14 December 2016